www.independent.co.uk

D1150954

WHO'S WHOSE?

A NO-NONSENSE GUIDE TO EASILY CONFUSED WORDS

By Philip Gooden

Copyright © 2004 by Philip Gooden

First published by Bloomsbury Publishing Plc, now published by A&C Black
Publishing Ltd.

The right of Philip Gooden to be identified as the author of this work has been
asserted by him in accordance with the Copyright, Designs and Patents Act 1998.

A CIP catalogue record for this book is available from the British Library.

All rights reserved. No part of this publication may be reproduced in any form or by
any means — graphic, electronic or mechanical, including photocopying, recording,
taping or information storage and retrieval systems — without the written
permission of A & C Black Publishers Limited.

'Who's Whose?' © Independent News & Media 2008
Cover design © Independent News & Media 2008
Printed in England by Cox & Wyman Ltd, Reading, Berkshire

Cover image: Clare Elsom/NB Illustration

NO-NONSENSE ENGLISH

SAVE OVER £10

If you enjoy this abridged version of *Who's Whose?* why not order the complete book and other Philip Gooden titles:

£7.99 • 978-07136-82342 • Paperback

**Winner of the
HRH Duke of Edinburgh English
Speaking Union English Language Book Award**

A lively and engaging exposé on the foreign words and phrases that populate our language. If you have ever been bamboozled by the use of a foreign word or phrase, or simply want to spice up your vocabulary with some well chosen *bons mots*, then this is the book for you.

£7.99 • 978-07136-85237 • Paperback

Ever had a Hitchcockian experience or met someone with a distinctly Ortonesque outlook on life? There are hundreds of words derived from real people who are famous - or infamous - enough to give their stamp to a movement, a way of thinking or acting, a style or even a mood. This is an essential guide to the better known or more intriguing of these terms.

£9.99 • 978-07136-75887 • Hardback

And a little something extra:

Covering everything from the politically incorrect to the seriously taboo, this humorous book offers over 3,000 ways to avoid speaking your mind! Subjects covered include crime, sins, sex, the body and its parts, clothing and nakedness, bodily functions and secretions, illness and injury, old age and death, work, poverty, government and politics, warfare and race.

£9.99 • 978-07136-78406 • Paperback

SPECIAL OFFER: ORDER ALL 4 BOOKS FOR £25

To order call 01256 302699 or email direct@macmillan.co.uk
For FREE p+p on UK orders and to take advantage of the 4 for £25 offer, **please quote code H94**

For more information, visit: **www.acblack.com/wordbooks**

INTRODUCTION

Who's or *whose*? *Disinterested* or *uninterested*? *Ameliorate* or *alleviate*?
Is there anybody who hasn't at some point had to consider, when faced
with a choice between these or other similar-sounding words, which one
will better convey the required shade of meaning? Or, more simply, hasn't
stopped to wonder which word is the right one?

All of us, in practice, choose the language which we use. And we choose
all the time, whether consciously or not. The expressions in an email will
be different from those used in a formal letter; the words said in the pub
aren't necessarily the same as the words heard in the workplace. Almost
everybody adjusts the register of his or her language, according to
circumstances and company. A lot of this may be instinctive, but it is an
instinct which is constantly being modified and refined. We learn about the
words we use as we go along.

English is a wealthy language. The number of words available to any
speaker or writer of it comfortably exceeds half a million, at least in theory.
Anybody who has a working knowledge of just 5 per cent of that total can
claim to have an extensive vocabulary, much more than is needed for
everyday purposes. Buried in this great heap of words are many duplicates or
near-duplicates, terms that mean the same or almost the same as other
terms. And, more deceptively, there are words that look or sound as though
they mean the same as others. This book is a guide to some of the most
frequent and interesting confusables in English – or confusibles (there's a
choice here too).

Anybody who writes about English usage needs to face the question:
Does it matter? Is the misuse – or abuse – of language truly important?
We generally manage to make our meaning clear, even if our vocabulary is
pretty basic, perhaps especially if it is pretty basic. Are slips of the tongue
where one says *less* instead of *fewer*, or uncertainties about whether to
write *phase* or *faze* really significant? Sometimes, the answer must be no.
Your listener or reader may not care about any mistake, may not even
notice any mistake. But, of course, the reverse is also true. That listener or
reader may notice, may care.

I wouldn't, however, want to base a defence of correct usage solely on
what others might think – that makes the whole business too nervy and
defensive. Speaking and writing English is about communicating with
others, naturally, but much of the benefit of using language well is for the
sake of the user. There is a great increase in confidence and, yes, an
increase in pleasure in saying what one wants to say, in having a firm grasp
of the intricacies of vocabulary – or some of the intricacies, since there will

always be that other half a million words or so to get familiar with. And English does not become much more intricate or tangled than in the area of confusables.

There are several reasons why all of us confuse words, whether often or occasionally. It may be no more than a matter of spelling (*advice/advise*) or uncertainty about which way round a term applies (*reliable/reliant*). At other times the distinction between expressions may be subtle (*defective/deficient*) or hard to pin down (*recourse/resource*). And there is yet another category where people assume a difference but where, in practice, none exists (*stanch* and *staunch*; *inoculate* and *vaccinate*). Confusables have always existed, of course, but reliance on the spellchecker, and the general speeding-up of the publishing process, mean that we see more and more confused spellings and usages in print.

Of course, the words in *Who's Whose?* are just the tip of the iceberg. Or – thinking of those half million or more still to go – the tip of the tip. But this is the part which is the most visible.

The entries in this book are organised alphabetically, sometimes with the more familiar form/spelling coming first (e.g. *bizarre/bazaar*). An opening sentence or two helps to outline the reason(s) why the two or more terms are mixed up. The main part of each entry defines the terms, with examples generally drawn from the newspapers, although with a few from other sources such as fiction. (Where I have not found particular usages I have made up examples.) At the end of each entry is an *Embarrassment rating* which rates – on a scale from nil (represented by OOO) through moderate (represented by ●❶O) to high (represented by ●●●) – the 'seriousness' of confusing the words under discussion. And finally, under the heading of 'How to avoid', there is some guidance on telling the confusables apart, how to avoid writing one for the other, etc.

In some cases the guidance may perhaps be trickier to recall than the original words, and I would always suggest that, in cases of doubt, the user should consult a dictionary or a reference book like this one rather than struggle with memory aids. Sometimes, the best advice that can be given over English usage is simply: be careful. And the next best is: use a dictionary. It helps, too, to be aware of words which are likely to cause you, or others, problems.

Philip Gooden

A A A A A

ABUSE *or* MISUSE

Two words which have a considerable overlap of meaning. Different contexts require the use of one rather than the other.

Of the two, *abuse* is the more serious term, constantly appearing in phrases like child *abuse* or *abuse* of power. To *abuse* means to 'make bad use of'. As noun or verb it can describe the physical (usually sexual), verbal or psychological mistreatment of others. When applied to drink and drugs, the word suggests an excessive, uncontrolled intake of the substance in question (arguably, people should really refer to alcohol misuse, but *abuse* is more attention-grabbing):

> *...new 'drinking warehouses' and superpubs are fuelling a culture of alcohol abuse.* (Daily Telegraph)

To *misuse* is to 'use for the wrong purpose'. The two words are often used interchangeably but there can be a useful distinction. To use a book as a doorstop is a *misuse* of it as an object, but to take the contents of that book and deliberately misrepresent what the author is saying would be an *abuse* of it. Another distinction is that an *abuse* is generally a conscious action while a *misuse* may be committed unawares. It's more forgivable, as in this example:

> *...it is not uncommon for any of us to misuse language when hoping to convey a truth.* (Daily Telegraph)

Embarrassment rating: ●●◐ To accuse someone of *misusing* something is a lot less offensive than accusing them of *abuse*, especially now that the word is so frequently linked to children.

How to avoid: Most people are very sensitive to the overtones of *abuse*, and will instinctively shy away from the word unless they feel it is really justified. This is particularly so in professional (i.e. social work) circles where, for example, substance *abuse* has now become *misuse*.

ACQUIESCE, ASSENT or AGREE

These three words occupy the same sort of area but have different shades of meaning.

To *acquiesce* is to 'consent without showing opposition':

He acquiesced in the plans although he had no part in making them.

To assent has a slightly formal tone to it and means to 'comply', to 'agree to' (usually without much eagerness). *Agree* covers these two senses but also extends to more positive meanings: to 'be of one mind with', 'be compatible with'.

Embarrassment rating: ◑○○ But a careful writer/speaker can convey enthusiasm – or the lack of it – by the right choice among these words.

How to avoid: There is perhaps not much to avoid here. It's more a matter of degrees of enthusiasm. *Acquiesce* and *assent* are terms more likely to occur in writing than speech (where they could sound pompous), and anyone using them on paper is likely to be aware of their shades of meaning. *Agree* can be conveniently neutral when put in writing, whereas we all know that, when spoken, it can convey anything between eagerness and a grudging acceptance.

ACTOR or ACTRESS

One of a group of word-pairs describing professions where the neutral form has traditionally been reserved for the male sex. The problem comes with the 'feminine' form of each pair, use of which is frequently seen now as not PC.

The tendency is to avoid words that designate the sex of the person carrying out a particular job, thus 'firefighter' is preferred to 'fireman'. An *actor* describes a person who acts on stage, film or TV, irrespective of sex:

First, there is the fact that she is generally considered an extremely bad actor indeed – chronic, even. (The Times)

(The difference between 'actor' and 'star' would make for an interesting little excursion – not all actors have star quality, but most stars refer to themselves as actors when they want to be taken seriously.)

Other art forms are also home to unisex terms like 'author', 'poet', 'sculptor'. There are feminine forms of some of these terms ('authoress', 'poetess') but they not only sound out of date but have a slightly patronising air, as if the women were merely dabbling in the activity. Even in ballet, the feminine 'ballerina' has generally been replaced by 'dancer'. In those few areas where men and women have long been on a more equal footing, the feminine form may sometimes be retained – waiter/waitress; steward/stewardess; headmaster/headmistress – although, as far as the last two are concerned, there is a preference now for the sexually unrevealing 'flight attendant', and 'principal' for the head of a school. Job advertisements, wary of accusations of discrimination, may also announce that they are looking for strange, hybrid beings called 'waitpersons' or 'postpersons'. One of the fields where the sex difference still holds is the host/hostess distinction. 'Hostess' leads a kind of double life: ultra-respectable at a dinner party but slightly sleazy in a clip-joint or nightclub. 'Host' can be used for either sex, however.

Embarrassment rating: ●○○ When it comes to actors, it depends if you're talking to a luvvie or a serious actor. The latter might just be offended, I suppose.

How to avoid: Play safe and refer to all artistic practitioners by the neutral form: actor, sculptor, etc. But it's difficult to believe that many people would naturally say 'waitperson' rather than 'waitress'.

AFFECT or EFFECT

Two words that sound very similar and which are frequently mixed up. To add to the confusion, the noun which relates to the main meaning of *affect* is *effect*.

As a verb affect means to 'have an impact on', 'make a difference to':

Peter's drinking affected his health more than his personality. (Independent)

Also, as a verb affect has the less usual meaning of to 'put on', to 'pretend':

Donovan wasn't ready to affect his Yorkshire accent at a press conference yesterday. (The Times)

To *effect* is to 'bring about', to 'carry through':

They effected the most dramatic transformation almost overnight.

In the next sentence *effect* has been used wrongly instead of affect:

Concern about job security now effects [should be **affects**] *everyone from mandarin to road sweeper.* (The Times)

The noun which relates to the verb *affect* and has the same general sense of 'impact' is not, as one might expect, *affect* but *effect*:

The harmful effects of cigarette smoking are now well established.

So the following are wrong:

And he had the same affect [should be **effect**] *on his players.* (Sun)

...the crash of 1929 had profound affects [should be **effects**] *on law and order.* (Independent on Sunday)

Embarrassment rating: ●○○ Almost everybody mixes up their *affects* and *effects* from time to time. The general sense of what you are writing is unlikely to be *affected*, but it's still a mistake.

How to avoid: *Affect* is the more common of the two verbs, so the chances are that it will be the right word if you are looking for a verb. However, if your sentence contains a word like 'change', 'transformation', 'improvement' then it is likely to be preceded by *effect*, i.e. 'bring about'. When it's the noun you want, *effect* will almost certainly be right (since the rarely found *affect* has the specialist, psychological sense of 'emotion' or 'desire'). But knowing whether you are looking for noun or verb depends on knowing parts of speech... There's no shortcut here. Just consult this book.

AGGRAVATE *or* ANNOY

These two words were separate once. But popular use has transferred the meaning of *annoy* to *aggravate*, so that it has become *annoy* with knobs on. Maybe it is the similarity of the word to 'aggression' that causes the error.

The primary meaning of *aggravate* is to 'make worse' – as in the following example, where it is balanced against the idea of making better or easing a situation:

> *It stands to reason that the Iraq venture was always going to aggravate not relieve the so-called War on Terror.* (The Times)

By contrast, *annoy* often means no more than 'irritate':

> *She was annoyed by the frequent interruptions to her work.*

Embarrassment rating: OOO Nil in speech but low to moderate in formal writing, since the principal sense of *aggravate* is still alive and well, although I suspect it will sooner or later be pushed to one side by the informal sense of 'deeply irritate'.

How to avoid: In formally correct English, you can *aggravate* a condition or a situation but not a person – therefore if an individual is the object of your *aggravation* the chances are that you are misusing the word.

ALLEVIATE *or* AMELIORATE

There's no particular trap here since these two are close in meaning; they are not absolutely identical, however.

To *alleviate* is to 'make lighter'. It's generally applied to moods, emotional burdens, pain, or states of mind:

> *...the various friends whose inconsolable grief at my departure is to be somewhat alleviated by the legacy of some trinket or other.* (The Times)

To *ameliorate* is to 'bring about an improvement'. The tendency is to use the word about physical conditions (illness, poverty, etc.):

> *...if they linked those machines up to a generator, it might produce enough juice... to sell back to the grid, which along with wind farms would certainly*

help ameliorate the looming energy crisis. (Observer)

That said, you could exchange the two words in the examples above without producing a significant change in meaning!

Embarrassment rating: ○○○

How to avoid: There are some situations where one word may simply 'feel' more appropriate than the other.

ALTERNATE *or* ALTERNATIVE

There's a clear distinction between these two, but they both contain the ideas of 'otherness' and 'change' and are frequently confused.

Alternative can be used as a noun or adjective, and indicates that a 'choice' is being offered. Originally the word was restricted to contexts where no more than two options were available, but it's often used now to indicate a wider range of choices:

Prime ministers are often unpopular; yet they can still win large general election victories if voters nevertheless believe the government is doing a better job than the alternatives. (Guardian)

Alternate is both adjective and verb. As an adjective, it means 'occurring by turns', 'every other':

We make deliveries in your area on alternate Thursdays.

As a verb, *alternate* means to 'shift from one thing to another, and then back again':

Her moods alternated between euphoria and gloom.

The adjectival form of alternate shouldn't be used as a substitute for *alternative*:

The city was an alternate [should be alternative] *target and was bombed two days earlier than planned.* (Guardian)

(This suggests that the city was bombed by turns with another target.)

Alternative also describes technology, medicine, comedy, etc. which is not mainstream.

Embarrassment rating: ●○○ , since the writer's or speaker's meaning may be obscured. This may not happen often, but there is a real difference between the sentence 'The boy spent alternate holidays with his father', meaning that he holidayed with his mother or someone else the rest of the time, and 'The boy spent alternative holidays with his father', meaning that they dropped in on a commune.

How to avoid: If in doubt which to use, try rephrasing the sentence. If a choice between two or more items is involved then *alternative* is the right word, but if time/frequency are in question then *alternate* is probably right.

AMEND *or* EMEND

Both verbs have very similar pronunciation and the same general sense but the second is used only in a very particular context.

To *amend* is to 'improve by changing or correcting':

President Bush has signalled that he will support amending the federal Constitution to prevent same-sex couples from getting married. (The Times)

To *emend* has the more restricted sense of 'make alterations in a written text':

She emended the proof copy before returning it to the printers.

(The nouns from each verb are *amendment* and *emendation*.)

Embarrassment rating: ●○○ There is a difference between *amending* a rule and *emending* it, since the second implies no more than making physical changes to the wording.

How to avoid: *Amend* has a much more general application and is likely to be the correct form/spelling. Only use *emend* and *emendation* where texts, drafts, etc. are concerned.

AMIABLE *or* AMICABLE

Both adjectives are to do with friendliness but have different applications.

Amiable means 'friendly', 'likeable':

He was popular for his easy-going and amiable manner.

Amicable means 'in a friendly spirit', and tends to be found in situations where differences of opinion have been resolved without a quarrel, or where bad relations might be expected:

They divorced 12 months later and all seemed amicable. (Daily Mirror)

Embarrassment rating: ●○○ But *amicable* is a more formal term than *amiable* and the context where one is used is not necessarily appropriate for the other.

How to avoid: *Amiable* is used of people and their manner, smiles, facial expressions and so on. *Amicable* applies rather to situations, understandings, agreements, etc.

AMNESTY *or* MORATORIUM

These two words are sometimes confused, probably because both refer to a specified period in which some normal process is suspended.

An *amnesty* is a 'general pardon' or describes a 'period in which crimes can be admitted to without penalty':

...the government renewed the amnesty offered to paramilitary organisations which decommission weapons. (Guardian)

A *moratorium* describes a 'stretch of time when an activity is halted'. It is often applied to the suspension of debt payment but has wider uses:

> *There has been little support from the conservation community for the Botswana government's four-year moratorium on lion hunting.* (Guardian)

Embarrassment rating: ●●○ If you know enough to employ these slightly specialist terms, you should know the difference between them. It would be incorrect to change them round in the examples above.

How to avoid: The organisation that campaigns for the rights of political prisoners and against state torture is called Amnesty. Less helpfully, *moratorium* derives from a Latin word meaning 'delay'. A clue, however, is that *moratorium* is generally followed by 'on'.

ANOINT *or* APPOINT

Two similar-sounding words which are to do with formally establishing someone in a position.

To *anoint* was originally to 'smear with oil as an act of consecration'. Anointing still takes place during the coronation of monarchs or the consecration of archbishops. But the word is quite widely used now in the sense of to 'install in an important position' – and the context doesn't have to be serious:

> *...the nation's favourite gay man and the* Radio Times's *recently anointed most powerful person in comedy* (Guardian)

To *appoint* is simply to 'select for a position':

> *She was appointed managing director at a relatively early age.*

Embarrassment rating: ●●○, if you say something like 'she was anointed managing director...' – unless you're being ironic.

How to avoid: Although *anoint* has moved away from royalty and gone downmarket, it shouldn't be used about everyday appointments.

ANTICIPATE *or* EXPECT

These two verbs are widely treated as if they were interchangeable but there is a useful difference in meaning between them.

To *anticipate* is not merely to believe that something will happen (i.e. expect), but to 'take some action to prevent or lessen the consequences of what will occur'. Where *expect* is largely passive:

> *They're expecting it to rain tomorrow.*

anticipate has more active overtones:

> *Anticipating rain, she took her umbrella with her.*

Embarrassment rating: ●○○, since so many people use *anticipate* when they really mean *expect*. It is worth trying to preserve this distinction, however, since there is no other single word in English which combines the idea of expectation and action in the way that *anticipate* does.

How to avoid: This is a question of precise use. Before using *anticipate* you should ask yourself whether the subject of the sentence has actually done anything to deal with whatever is expected. If they haven't, then the simple *expect* would be more correct.

APPRAISE *or* APPRISE

These bureaucratic-sounding words are quite easy to mix up, not only because of their similar sound and spelling but because they can occur in the same sort of context.

The verb *appraise* means to 'sum up', to 'estimate the value or quality of' something or somebody (not usually in a monetary sense):

...his intense skull and cold blazing eyes appraise you with a look of narcissistic derision. (Spectator)

(The noun is *appraisal* – a pseudo-technical-sounding word now most often applied to the way in which employees are assessed by their bosses.)

To *apprise* (slightly formal rather than in everyday use) is to 'give notice to', 'tell':

[Sylvia] Plath, who has already apprised her husband of two earlier suicide attempts, resents his way with the ladies, and begins to suspect that he is having an affair. (Guardian)

Embarrassment rating: ●●○ The two words have nothing to do with each other, as is shown by comparing the sentences 'She was apprised of the situation' and 'She appraised the situation'. To confuse them is to show ignorance

How to avoid: As a rule of thumb *appraise* cannot be followed by 'of', whereas *apprise* has to be. There are simpler and perhaps preferable expressions for these two – 'judge' or 'assess' for *appraise* and 'tell' or 'inform' for *apprise*. Use these if in doubt.

ARBITER, ARBITRATOR *or* MEDIATOR

These three terms, all describing people who assess situations and sort out problems, are sometimes used interchangeably but they have distinct shades of meaning.

An *arbiter* is an 'umpire', one who lays down the law or sets a standard of taste. The word is often found in connection with fashion or public opinion:

> Her treatment also raises the danger that populist newspapers like the Sun
> ...will become the arbiters of public confidence. (Guardian)

An *arbitrator* is 'someone brought in to settle a dispute'. This word, rather
than *arbiter*, tends to be used in trade disputes and the law:

> Mr Justice Popplewell... once sued a paper for libel for saying he was asleep
> when he wasn't. The arbitrator, the late Lord (Gareth) Williams QC, awarded
> him £7,500. (Guardian)

A *mediator* is an 'individual who acts as a go-between', sometimes when
two or more parties are in disagreement but often simply to keep things
running smoothly:

> Mikhail Fradkov, the new prime minister, is the former Russian envoy to the EU
> and will act as a mediator to improve relations. (Guardian)

Embarrassment rating: ●◐○○ There is a blurring of meaning between the
first two, but even so one should not refer to, say, an *arbitrator* of fashion.
How to avoid: *Arbiter* can be used generally, although it contains the notion
of judgement which may not always be appropriate for the *mediator's* role.

ARCHETYPE *or* STEREOTYPE

A pair of words which are to do with pattern-makers and models. The
difference between them is that between an antique and a reproduction.

An *archetype* is the 'original model from which copies are produced':

> Hollywood... also captured the world's imagination with a whole series of
> American archetypes: the cowboy, the gangster, the little tramp. (Telegraph)

Almost by definition there can only be one *archetype* for each pattern but
the adjectival form of the word – *archetypal* – is very often used to mean
one of many rather than the 'first' of many. In this sense, 'typical' or
'standard' or even 'stereotypical' is more accurate:

> Even the hardiest club cricketer is likely to enter the archetypal [**stereotypical** would
> be better] ramshackle village pavilion with a wrinkled nose. (Daily Telegraph)

A *stereotype* is a 'clichéd image', 'something which conforms completely to
a standard pattern', and there is usually a negative shading to the word (as
there is to the verb *stereotype* and the adjective *stereotypical*):

> Terence Stamp leaves no stone unturned as he delivers every American's idea
> of the classic English servant stereotype. (Daily Mirror)

Embarrassment rating: ●○○ But it is preferable to be clear as to whether
you're talking about an original, an *archetype*, or the copy, a *stereotype*.
How to avoid: The 'arch-' part of *archetype* may suggest something high
and so outstanding, original. If you want to sound critical rather than
neutral, use *stereotype*.

ASSUMPTION *or* PRESUMPTION

There is no real difference between the verbs assume and presume in the sense of to 'take for granted' but there is a distinction between their noun forms, *assumption* and *presumption*.

An *assumption* can be a 'supposition which isn't supported by evidence'; 'false' is the adjective often partnered with it and, even if it turns out to be correct, it has more the sense of a 'guess':

...the assumption was that, following his messy public divorce in a Cape Town court, she picked him up and dusted him down. (Daily Telegraph)

A *presumption* has more the sense of a 'probability', i.e. it is more than guesswork:

Every village these days is set within a so-called developmental envelope, which governs planning decisions. Within the village envelope, there is a presumption that some degree of development will be allowed.
(Daily Telegraph)

Under English law, courts work on the *presumption* of innocence rather than the *assumption* of it

(*Presume* can also carry the sense of 'be bold enough to', as in 'I wouldn't presume to tell you how to do your job'. Another related sense attached to *presumption* is 'arrogance', 'insolence'.)

Embarrassment rating: ◐○○ But the careful user will observe the shade of difference between a belief which isn't much more than a guess (*assumption*) and one which has, say, past experience to back it up (*presumption*).

How to avoid: See above. A *presumption* is a *rea*sonable belief; an assumption could be *su*spect.

ASSURE, ENSURE *or* INSURE

These three verbs, all containing some idea of 'guarantee', are related but have different applications.

To *assure* is to 'guarantee', to 'give certainty to someone':

They did their best to assure him that he was welcome.

To *ensure* is to 'make something safe or certain':

Careful preparation helped to ensure the success of the expedition.

To *insure* is to 'protect oneself (financially) against loss or damage':

We've insured for the trip after last year's disaster.

(The noun *assurance* can describe 'anything which is intended to inspire confidence or belief ' such as an encouraging remark. When used in the context of the insurance market, *assurance* relates to those policies which cover an individual's life and pay the beneficiaries on his or her death. *Insurance* can also be used to describe [life] *assurance* policies, and is applied to everything else against which one can insure: accident, fire, theft, etc.)

Embarrassment rating: ●◐○ If there's any confusion, it's likely to occur with the first two. The difference is shown by 'The general assured his men that their superior skills would ensure victory'.

How to avoid: *Insure* and *insurance* are always connected to financial payments or some other security against disaster. *Assure* and *assurance* and reassurance are usually related to words or symbolic gestures. To *ensure* (there is no noun equivalent) suggests the taking of physical measures to achieve something.

AURAL *or* ORAL

Both words are adjectives with a near-identical pronunciation and both are often connected with types of exam. Any problems over use are likely to be connected with the less familiar *aural* and to occur in speech rather than writing.

Aural means 'of the ear':

In the secular songs of England's supreme composer, Henry Purcell, romance is given its consummate aural shape. (The Times)

Oral means 'relating to the mouth':

Video on-demand technology installed in dentists' chairs is the latest attempt to make oral surgery appear less of an ordeal. (The Times)

As a noun, *oral* describes an examination where the candidate gives spoken answers. Confusion sometimes arises when the words are used in this context. An *aural* examination in French would test the candidate's ability to <u>hear and understand</u> that language when spoken. But a French *oral* tests the candidate's capacity to <u>speak</u> the language.

Embarrassment rating: ●○○ Confusion over which is meant in speech is easily resolved. To take one example: no one is likely to think that *oral* sex refers to the ear – if *aural* sex existed it would presumably be the same as phone sex.

How to avoid: Some speakers distinguish between the two words by pronouncing the first syllable of *aural* to rhyme with 'ow'. Try remembering that an *or*ator speaks, or *or*ates, whereas an *au*dience listens.

B B B B B

BAIL *or* BALE

There are so many meanings associated with this simple pair of words that uncertainty over which form to use on which occasion is almost bound to occur.

Bail is a noun and verb with several meanings. An accused person will obtain *bail*, or be *bailed*, in court, i.e. 'gain release from custody before trial by providing some security' (usually financial) which will be forfeit if the defendant disappears. To *bail* also means to 'clear water out of' something, and to 'parachute out of an aircraft'. And finally, cricket stumps are topped by *bails*.

 Bale can also be used as a verb in two of the senses above (*baling* water; *baling* out of a crashing aircraft). As a noun *bale* means a 'bundle' (a *bale* of cotton); as a verb, to 'do up in bundles' (*baling* hay).

Embarrassment rating: ●○○ As indicated, these words not only have a variety of meanings but can, in some contexts, be used interchangeably.

How to avoid: *Bale* is the more adaptable form, covering everything from bundles to aircraft escapes. The only places where the *bail* spelling must be used are in a legal setting ('Bail was set at £20,000') and on the cricket field.

BENEFICENT, BENEFICIAL, BENEVOLENT *or* BENIGN

These words have positive overtones connected with the doing of good but they crop up in different surroundings, and the wrong choice can sound odd.

Beneficent is a fairly high-flown word meaning 'kind or charitable' and tends to describe people and their actions or outlook:

 It set the seal on an event of joyous anarchy, as if the composer's beneficent shade were with us... (Daily Telegraph)

Beneficial can mean simply 'useful', as in 'a beneficial exchange of views', but its most usual context is probably to do with 'promoting health or well-being':

The doctor suggested that a change of scene would be beneficial.

Benevolent falls somewhere between *beneficent* and *benign*, in that it can describe somebody who's merely 'well disposed' towards others as well as suggesting actions that are more positively 'charitable' – it's in this second sense that societies once incorporated *benevolent* into their titles, although any charity setting up now would avoid the word since it has overtones of patronage.

Benign, with the sense of 'kindly', is more to do with attitude than action (a *benign* smile, a *benign* presence) and has a specialist sense in describing a 'non-cancerous' growth – the opposite of 'malign/malignant'.

Embarrassment rating: ●○○, since this is a question of shades of meaning. However, to describe a medicine as 'benevolent' instead of 'beneficial' or to refer to a charity donor as 'benign' rather than 'benevolent' would suggest an uncertain grasp of language.

How to avoid: *Benevolent* (showing goodwill) is the opposite of 'malevolent' (showing ill-will). *Beneficial* is linked with effects, therapies, diets, and is often followed by 'to', with the sense 'of *benefi*t to'. *Beneficent* is extremely rare so unlikely to trouble you. But generally only the context of the word, and some sensitivity to its overtones, will tell you which to use.

BESIDE *or* BESIDES

These two everyday words are often used as though they were completely interchangeable. They aren't.

Beside means 'next to' ('the table stood *beside* the window'). *Besides* means 'in addition to' ('*besides* the table, the room contained several chairs') and 'apart from' ('*besides* the table and chairs, the room was empty'). *Besides*, generally followed by a comma, also has the sense of 'moreover' ('*Besides*, there was nothing to be seen in the room!').

Embarrassment rating: ◑○○ There is a potential ambiguity in a sentence such as 'Beside the table, several chairs were found in the room', where it may not be clear whether the writer means that the chairs were near the table or that they were simply scattered about the place. Technically the first interpretation is the correct one.

How to avoid: If you mean 'by the side of' then put *beside*. Use *besides* for anything else.

BON VIVANT *or* BON VIVEUR

Two terms, apparently from French, which have a humorously sophisticated air to them and sound almost the same. They're not. *Bon viveur* is the one more often found but *bon vivant* is the one more often intended.

To take the more usual one first: a *bon viveur* is a 'pleasure-lover', a 'man about town'. Oddly, the original expression isn't used by the French ('nom de plume' is another example of this). Perhaps because of its fake-Frenchness, bon viveur has a rather dated naughtiness about it. Think of winks, nudges and twirled moustaches.

> *An 'emotional' court hearing in London revealed the tangled love life of the screen-writer and notorious bon viveur, who married three times and embarked on a love affair with Miss Minutolo in his 70s.* (The Times)

Just to confuse things, the term *bon vivant* is used in France with the meaning of 'jovial', although its feminine form *bonne vivante* is not found there – perhaps because joviality isn't regarded as a feminine attribute by the French? Anyway, in correct 'British' usage a *bon vivant* is a 'good companion' and 'someone who has a discriminating taste in food and drink':

> *...as any bon vivant will tell you, you rarely expect anything [in a station buffet] other than a smeared glass of gassy lager and an indigestible sausage roll when close to rolling stock.* (Daily Telegraph)

Embarrassment rating: ●◐○ , because if you want to impress by using these phrases you should know the difference between them.

How to avoid: Anybody wanting a word to convey a 'good-bloke-who-likes-a-drink-or-two', which is what *bon viveur* is generally taken to mean, should probably be using *bon vivant*. But then someone will say, 'Don't you mean a *bon viveur*?' or tell the speaker off for pedantry. Personally, I wouldn't use either expression.

BORN *or* BORNE

This is a tricky pair to get right, as the switch from the version without an 'e' to the one spelled with an 'e' sometimes seems almost arbitrary.

Borne is the past participle form of the verb to bear. It is applied to the carrier:

> *Used to guns, he had borne arms almost from the time he learned to walk.*

or to the thing or person carried:

> *So we beat on, boats against the current, borne back ceaselessly into the past.* (*Scott Fitzgerald*, The Great Gatsby)

When *bear* is used in the sense of to 'give birth', the form *borne* is used if the mother is the subject of the sentence:

She had borne him four children.

Otherwise the correct form is *born*:

Four children were born to her/Charles Dickens was born in Rochester.

It's quite easy to lose your bearings over *born/e*, as the following demonstrates:

This mistake is typical not of Conservatives but of the Left – borne [should be born] of the notion that a society is like a machine... (The Times)

Embarrassment rating: ●●○ This seems to me a genuinely awkward distinction, and so any error is fairly forgivable. Also, the meaning of the sentence is unlikely to be impaired by any slip.

How to avoid: If the writer can substitute 'carried', then the *borne* spelling will be correct. (This test works for the *Times* quotation above, since 'carried' <u>cannot</u> be substituted and therefore *born* should have been used.) When it comes to birth or babies, remember that *borne* is only usable where the mother is the subject; otherwise it's *born*.

BRAVADO *or* BRAVERY

These two are related but distinct, and should not be confused.

Like a cheap cracker, *bravado* goes off with a big bang to reveal nothing inside. Having the sense of a 'display of bravery', it shades into an 'aggressive showing off':

The main characteristic of teenage boys is bravado. (Daily Telegraph)

Bravery is the genuine article, 'courage':

...the ingenuity and bravery of the young airmen who dug a 330-ft tunnel out of the notorious prison camp have passed into modern mythology.
(Daily Telegraph)

Embarrassment rating: ●●●, since *bravado* is generally pejorative while *bravery* is complimentary.

How to avoid: Beware *bravado* unless you wish to cast aspersions.

BREACH *or* BREECH

Two words with a one-letter difference. Vague associations between 'openings', 'guns' and 'trousers' may encourage this confusion!

A *breach* is an 'opening' – as in the famous speech which Shakespeare gave to King Henry V, 'Once more unto the breach, dear friends'.
Metaphorically, it is a 'break in a contract' or a 'breakdown in relations between two groups':

...[he] also had to ensure that no breach occurred between Danish amateurs and professionals in the field. (The Times)

Breech describes the 'part of a gun behind the barrel' or the 'back or buttocks' (hence *breech* delivery, when the baby emerges buttocks- or feet-first). Apart from its connection with firearms, the word tends to appear in its plural form of *breeches*, meaning 'trousers'. The word is old-fashioned, of course, and specifically describes leggings which only reach to the knee:

A gloomy-looking Lord Falconer of Thoroton, the lord chancellor desperate to abandon his wig and breeches... (Guardian)

This second spelling should not be used when *breach* is meant:

...into this information breech [should be *breach*] *have leapt a whole raft of new-wave space capitalists...* (Guardian)

Embarrassment rating: ●●◑ , because *breach* is a common word – and if you put *breech* in error, then unavoidable images of climbing into a gun or a pair of trousers come to mind.

How to avoid: A *breach* is a *break*, and may be literal or metaphorical. If you are referring to *breech* or *breeches* you must be talking about a concrete object, e.g. part of a rifle.

BROACH *or* BROOCH

The second word is probably more usual than the first, yet is sometimes misspelled perhaps because the '-oa-' form looks more familiar, by analogy with 'coach' or 'poach'.

Broach, a verb, generally occurs in two contexts: to *broach* a topic, to 'introduce' it into conversation, often with the suggestion of difficulty:

...clients on her assertiveness training courses see broaching such matters with their bosses as an enormous emotional challenge. (Guardian)

and – less often – to broach a *bottle* (i.e. 'open' it).

Brooch, a noun, is an 'ornamental clasp':

Across her chest she wore a diamond brooch in the shape – and almost the size – of a tree branch. (Observer)

(Both words are pronounced in the same way, to rhyme with 'coach'.)

Embarrassment rating: ●●○ The general mistake (putting *broach* for *brooch*) is fairly easily made and will not affect the sense. It is a basic spelling error though and best avoided.

How to avoid: *Broach* is always a verb and so will be preceded by a subject, noun or pronoun, and usually followed by 'topic', 'question', etc. *Brooch* is a noun only and so will tend to have 'a/the' in front of it.

C C C C C

CAN *or* MAY

Two very simple words which are used interchangeably but which can – or may – convey subtly different meanings.

Can denotes ability:

  She can speak five languages.

(but is often used in the sense of 'has permission':

  She's just been told she can come on the trip).

May indicates possibility:

  It may rain tomorrow.

and permission:

  You may leave when the job's finished.

There is a small potential ambiguity in a sentence like the one above, which could mean 'You might take it into your head to leave…'.

There is a stronger ambiguity in a sentence like 'He may drive across'. Context and tone of voice will tell the listener whether it's a matter of permission or possibility.

Embarrassment rating: OOO Long, long ago a pedantic teacher or parent might pick on a child's question 'Can I do X?' by saying 'Of course you *can* do X. What you mean is, *may* you do it?' But no one talks like this any more, do they?

How to avoid: Despite the above, it's sometimes worth considering in formal writing the distinction between *can* and *may*. Do you want to imply capability or permission?

CAPTIVATE *or* CAPTURE

Two words which contain the idea of an 'involuntary taking over'. Confusion may occur because, while a *captive* is a prisoner and captivity is imprisonment, the verb to *captivate* has quite different and more pleasant associations.

To *captivate* is to 'fascinate', to 'enchant':

Much like the rest of the crowd, he was captivated by González's oratory...
(Guardian)

(The distinction needs to be observed between the adjectival forms *captive* and *captivated*: a *captive* audience is one which can't get out; a *captivated* audience is one which is delighted to be there.)

To *capture* is to 'gain control of '. Although frequently used in a neutral sense ('to *capture* someone's attention') it also carries the meaning of to 'seize by force':

The prisoner was captured after five hours on the run.

Embarrassment rating: ●●◐ , since neither of these words can be substituted for the other. A prisoner might be *captivated* by his freedom, but he wouldn't be so delighted after being *captured* and returned to *captivity*.

How to avoid: This is quite a tricky set of distinctions – particularly that between *captive* and *captivated* – since the boundaries between the words are blurred. Some rhyming association between *captivate* and 'fascinate' may help.

CELIBATE *or* CHASTE

These two are sometimes treated as an interchangeable pair of heavenly twins but there are differences between them.

Celibate is an adjective or noun which describes someone 'unmarried'. Because the word was most often applied in the past to those in religious orders who were necessarily unmarried and because – a big because, this – the friars, monks and nuns were supposed to lead a sexually abstinent life, *celibacy* became equated with a sex-free existence. This may be a lifestyle choice now, especially in the US, where young people are encouraged to save themselves for marriage by remaining *celibate*. But over in unreformed old Britain there can still be something a bit high-minded and priggish about the word:

After his marriage broke up Aitken claimed to be living the life of a celibate who could not conceive of a relationship with another woman. (Guardian)

Chaste doesn't have to mean 'going without sex', although this is generally implied. It carries the sense of 'modest', 'restrained':

...they find themselves aimlessly passing the time in a Tokyo hotel, unable to relate to the alien Japanese culture but finding a deep, though chaste, connection with each other. (Guardian)

Embarrassment rating: ●○○ Chastity, so highly valued in Victorian novels (at least for the heroine), has become something of a liability. I suspect many people would rather be 'accused' of being *celibate* than *chaste* since, as suggested above, this can be seen as a matter of lifestyle rather than morality.

How to avoid: *Celibate* can be applied to an individual's current status – it does not imply a *chaste* past or future, and this second term should be reserved for individuals or circumstances that really deserve the accolade of modesty and purity.

CENSOR, CENSURE, CENSER *or* SENSOR

Four words of quite similar sound and spelling. The first two are connected by ideas of disapproval; the second two are physical objects.

As a verb *censor* is to 'check material so as to assess its suitability for 'publication' ' (this covers letters, film, TV, etc.). Wartime provides a natural context:

> *All the officer patients in the ward were forced to censor letters written by all the enlisted-men patients...* (*Joseph Heller*, Catch-22)

The person who does this is the *censor* (as in the British Board of Film Censors [BBFC] though the last word usually appears now as Classification).

To *censure* is to 'judge unfavourably', to 'rebuke', while the noun carries the same meaning of 'harsh criticism':

> *I know one woman who had to put her make-up on outside, to escape the censure of her strict, puritanical eight-year-old daughter.* (Independent)

A *censer* is a 'vessel for burning incense':

> *Sordi discovered his comic vocation when, as an altar boy in Rome, he raised giggles when he waved the censer too boisterously.* (Guardian)

And a sensor is an 'electrical device for registering sound, movement, etc.', usually installed for security.

Embarrassment rating: ●●○ Moderate if you confuse any one of these four with the other. Despite the overtones of the word, a *censor* does not *censure* material; he/she merely assesses its suitability for publication, etc. And neither word has any link to incense-burning or to burglar alarms!

How to avoid: The spelling of *censor* can be checked against censorship. The 'u' in censure can be linked with the 'u' in equivalent words like rebuke or judge. The *censer* is for burning in*cense*. And a *sensor senses* what is going on around it.

CEREMONIAL *or* CEREMONIOUS

Both adjectives derive from *ceremony* but they have different meanings and applications.

Ceremonial means 'with the proper ceremony or ritual':

After the peace treaty was signed, there was a ceremonial exchange of pens.

By contrast, *ceremonious* conveys a note of criticism and means 'overconcerned with ceremony' and therefore 'pompous':

His ceremonious manner made it clear that we should feel privileged to meet him.

Embarrassment rating: ●OO The chances are that the context will make the meaning clear, even if the wrong word is used.

How to avoid: *Ceremonial* tends to be applied to events or things like costumes; *ceremonious*, like pompous, is used about people and their behaviour.

CHAFE *or* CHAFF

Two slightly out-of-the-ordinary words where an additional 'f' can produce a difference in meaning.

To *chafe* – pronounced with a long 'a' – is to 'fret or wear by rubbing'. It can have a physical application (*chafed* skin) or a mental one. If a person *chafes* (at, against or under something) it means that he/she is resentful and uncomfortable on account of some external circumstance:

Wyndham had spent years chafing under the demands of the US pulp magazines he had written for under the name John Beynon. (Guardian)

As a noun *chaff* – pronounced with a short 'a' – has several meanings. It describes 'corn husks' (i.e., the useless part) and is widely used in the phrase 'sorting the wheat from the chaff'. *Chaff* is the metal foil scattered by fighter planes to deceive enemy radar. And, more generally, it describes 'anything which is worthless'.

As a verb, to *chaff* is to 'make fun of' (in a gentle way):

...cuddling his fragile mother and chaffing his once-feared father, now 85. (Daily Telegraph)

Don't get the two confused. In this next sentence, the weights were apparently teasing the expert's thighs:

The unfortunate expert suffered chaffing [should be chafing] *to his thighs from the weights.* (Independent)

Embarrassment rating: ●OO Unintended humour may result if the wrong spelling is used, as above.

How to avoid: *Chafe* recalls other painful verbs with a long 'a' such as 'scrape', 'grate' and 'abrade'. Like some other words with a double-letter ending – 'dross', 'fluff' – *chaff* describes something of little value.

CHILDISH *or* CHILDLIKE

Two words which obviously relate to childhood yet which aren't usually applied to children themselves. One is insulting, the other is a potential compliment. Which is which?

Childish is used about adults in a critical sense, and describes behaviour which is 'non-adult', 'petulant', 'spoilt' – all the things which adults are supposed to have grown out of. *Childish* is the antithesis of 'grown-up':

Even in his 30s he had childish tastes in food, preferring dishes that were bland or sweet.

Childlike is also applied to adults but this time often in approval, as it describes not so much behaviour as responses such as surprise and delight, or qualities like simplicity and trust – things that allegedly come more easily to children. *Childlike* is the opposite of 'worldly', 'cynical':

...he attends most games and displays an almost childlike pleasure at the exciting match-day atmosphere at Stamford Bridge. (Daily Telegraph)

Embarrassment rating: ●●○, if you mean to express approval and use *childish* in error for *childlike*. That said, plenty of people wouldn't be too pleased to be described as *childlike*, either.

How to avoid: Both words need careful handling. *Childish* is a particularly patronising term.

CHORD *or* CORD

Both words were originally to do with lines and strings, and were interchangeable. There's a distinction in meaning now, but some association between strings and music makes for uncertainty over which one to use in which context.

A *chord* refers to 'two or more musical notes sounded together', and is the spelling to use in sentences such as:

The opening chords of the symphony rang through the hall.

For all non-musical senses, the *cord* spelling can be used. The 'thick string' for tying parcels; the umbilical *cord*; the vocal *cords* (never *chords*); the spinal *cord* (but sometimes spinal *chord*).

Embarrassment rating: ●○○ But any written reference to umbilical *chords* somehow suggests music composed for a birth, and *vocal* chords would be ambiguous (because it might refer to the cords in the throat or to a musical sound).

How to avoid: For anything connected to music, *chord* (as in *chora*l) is likely to be all right: use *cord* for everything else.

CLIMAX or CRESCENDO

The second of these two words is regularly used in the sense of the first, although this is not its primary dictionary meaning.

Climax means 'culmination' and applies to the end-point and/or the most exciting moments in music, books, films and other forms of story-telling – and sex. No difficulty with the definition of *climax*. It's *crescendo* that causes problems. In fact it is quite rare to find *crescendo* used in its correct sense of 'increasing loudness':

> *One of the marvellous things about Augusta is that you know when anyone big is coming because you hear this murmur, which grows in a crescendo of cheers...* (quoted in the Daily Telegraph)

More usual is the application of *crescendo* to mean 'climax' or 'high point':

> *Takeover speculation reached a crescendo [should be climax] this weekend...* (Daily Telegraph)

(The plural of *crescendo* is *crescendos*.)

Embarrassment rating: ●◐○ There are some uses, or misuses, where people simply vote with their feet and nothing said by any careful user or pedant – if the two can be separated – is going to change things. The 'disinterested/uninterested' distinction is one such example. So is *climax/crescendo*. This 'mistake' is so well established that the newer meaning is driving out the proper one. Music specialists will continue to understand *crescendo* but for the rest of us there will soon be no single word to describe a growing noise.

How to avoid: Restrict the use of crescendo to a noise, musical or otherwise, which is actually getting louder.

COLLUDE, CONNIVE or CONSPIRE

These words share the common idea of plotting, but they have different shades of meaning and care needs to be taken before applying them to anybody.

To *collude* is to 'conspire with', especially in fraud. One of the parties in a collusion is likely to be on the 'inside' and so betraying his/her employers or colleagues:

> *The... security fear is of the croupier colluding with a customer.* (The Times)

To *connive*, meaning to 'plot', is a less critical term. It can suggest turning a blind eye to another's unofficial or illicit activities, or a slightly underhand working together, as here:

> *Your staff will always connive at presenting [a member of the Royal Family] as a dutiful grafter.* (Observer)

Conspire, once again to 'plot', is the strongest of these three terms and tends to be restricted to criminal or treasonous contexts.

Embarrassment rating: ●○○ These are all words of condemnation. But *conniving* is relatively mild, while to *collude* or to *conspire* have distinctly dubious, not to say criminal, overtones.

How to avoid: The stronger the 'offence', the more justified is the use of *collude* or *conspire*. Remember that people connive *at* something but collude *in* it with someone, or they conspire *to do* it with someone.

COMMON *or* MUTUAL

Two words which contain the ideas of sharing and exchange. The confusion between them is an old chestnut of usage dictionaries.

The difference between *common* and *mutual* is perhaps more apparent than real but it is nicely illustrated in:

> The common ground [which] Castleford, Wakefield and Featherstone Rovers, the third party, share is mutual loathing... (The Times)

Common means 'shared', 'held jointly', as in *common* knowledge.

Mutual describes something which is 'reciprocated'; in the example above, a feeling of loathing which each of the three teams involved in the Rugby League gives out and receives back from the other two. But *mutual* can also be used in the sense of 'held in common', e.g. *mutual* funds.

Embarrassment rating: ◑○○ There used to be a kind of nit-picking pedantry – the kind that underlies some of this book, perhaps – which would pick up on any confusion between *common* and *mutual*. But it was Charles Dickens who called his novel *Our Mutual Friend*, and what was good enough for him... Anyway, this is a usage which has long found general acceptability. In fact, had Dickens called the novel *Our Common Friend* the title would have been ambiguous (Our Vulgar Friend?). So the pedants were never more than half-right.

How to avoid: If you really want *mutual* to mean 'reciprocated' it may be better to use the second word, otherwise *common* may be understood.

COMPELLING, COMPULSIVE *or* COMPULSORY

Three words deriving from *compel/compulsion*, which fit different contexts.

The adjectives *compelling* and *compulsive* are close in meaning when applied to experiences or processes: a *compelling* or *compulsive* book or TV programme is one that is 'irresistible' and so highly readable or viewable.

When applied to a person, *compulsive* is usually a pejorative term describing someone who is 'in the grip of strong drive to behave in a certain way': a *compulsive* thief, a *compulsive* gambler. This kind of *compulsion* comes from inside the individual.

By contrast, *compulsory* (which is never used to describe an individual) applies to something which is 'obligatory' and imposed from outside:

> *The reason that ties are in... is that so few of us have to wear them any more that we have started to see them as a fun thing rather than a boring compulsory thing.* (The Times)

Embarrassment rating: ●●○ , if you confuse the first two when describing another person. Many of us would like to have *compelling* personalities but be less pleased if referred to as having *compulsive* ones.

How to avoid: If you are using *compulsive* about an individual, then the word must relate to some activity, and usually an undesirable one.

COMPLEMENT *or* COMPLIMENT

This is a very familiar pair of confusables in all its forms (including *complementary/complimentary*). The words have a one-letter difference but share the same pronunciation, and an underlying sense of something given or added.

As a noun *complement* is the 'number which will make complete' (as in a 'ship's complement') or an 'addition which makes for rightness or wholeness':

> *For the British, chips are the right complement to fried fish.*

The verb *complement* describes the process of adding something to 'make complete':

> *Almond's tight bouffant perfectly complemented the stripped-down primal throb of the duo's music...* (Guardian)

Compliment, whether noun or verb, is 'praise':

> *She complimented him on his skill in cooking.*

The usual mistake is to use this word when the other (the 'e' one) is intended:

> *The first of two movies being shown to compliment* [should be **complement**] *the Wild West [season]...* (Independent)

But in the following example the writer meant *compliment* and used the other one:

> *...the ultimate Yorkshire complement* [should be **compliment**]: *"This one's not bad."* (Independent)

The confusion extends to the adjectival forms *complementary* and *complimentary*, whose meanings are connected to the noun and verb definitions given above.

Embarrassment rating: ●●○ , because this is a common mistake. It will irritate, though.

How to avoid: *Complement* is connected to the idea of completeness: note the 'e's in the middle and end of each word. *Compliment* is praise: they share an 'i' in the middle.

COMPRISE *or* CONSIST

These two verbs have more or less the same sense, both being to do with the elements that make up a whole, but confusion comes over the way in which each fits into a sentence.

Both *comprise* and *consist* mean to 'include', to 'be formed of ', but *consist* is always followed by 'of' or 'in':

The New Testament consists of 27 books.

He claimed that the answer to falling sales consisted in cutting prices.

Comprise cannot always be used in place of *consist of* but, where it is, it must stand alone, without 'of ' or 'in':

The New Testament comprises 27 books.

'Comprised of' is frequently found but still wrong:

'Over half of the building is actually comprised [should be **the building actually consists**] *of thatched roof.'* (Radio 4)

Embarrassment rating: ●●○ The almost invariable mistake is the one in the final example ('comprised of'), and this grates on many people.

How to avoid: If in doubt, avoid *comprise* altogether. It can usually be replaced with a simpler formula such as 'made up of' or 'include' or, alternatively, left out altogether (e.g. 'Over half the building is actually thatched roof.').

CONTRADICTION *or* PARADOX

There is an overlap of meaning between these two, but though all *paradoxes* have a contradictory element to them, not all *contradictions* are *paradoxes*.

A *contradiction* is a 'denial' in speech or an 'inconsistency' in a viewpoint:

Does anybody still believe there is a contradiction between liking art and committing foul deeds? (Daily Telegraph)

If you contradict yourself you may be accused of fuzzy thinking, but to express a *paradox* suggests a more ingenious and agile state of mind since it is a 'statement which appears to be contradictory but which, when examined more closely, contains some truth'. A *contradiction* usually arises by accident while a *paradox* is the deliberate formulation of an unusual point of view:

> *This has much to do with [Audrey] Hepburn's on-screen persona – the paradox is that she radiates youth, yet seems older than her years.*
> (Daily Telegraph)

Embarrassment rating: ●○○ But to term something a *paradox* is to give it a kind of intellectual status, while to call it a *contradiction* is to disparage it.

How to avoid: Reserve *paradox* for those situations which justify the word. A simple clash or contrast is not a *paradox*.

CREDIBLE, CREDITABLE *or* CREDULOUS

Three words connected with ideas of belief and trust, but with quite different meanings.

Credible means 'believable':

> *He had some extraordinary things to say but his quiet manner made them credible.*

The adjective is very widely used now to suggest not so much that something exists (i.e. is not a fiction), but that it should be taken seriously, as in 'a credible fighting force'. (The associated noun is *credibility* with the sense of 'believability'.)

Creditable means 'worth praising', with the slight suggestion that whatever is to be praised has been achieved in difficult circumstances:

> *Despite her ankle injury, she put up a very creditable performance.*

(The noun equivalent is *credit* with the sense of 'honour', 'worth', and frequently with a financial application, as in *credit* limit, *credit* facilities, etc.)

Credulous means 'easily deceived', too 'ready to accept whatever people say':

> *He made a living selling suspect designer perfumes to credulous tourists.*

(The associated noun, not often used, is *credulousness*. *Credulity* has the same meaning and is more often found, especially in phrases such as 'strain/stretch someone's credulity'.)

Embarrassment rating: ●●○, since one of these words (*creditable*) confers a degree of praise; one is somewhere between favourable and neutral (*credible*); and the other (*credulous*) is a pejorative term. Putting one in error for another changes your meaning.

How to avoid: *Credible* usually applies to individuals, either to their stories or their capabilities (think of the opposite, 'incredible'); *creditable* describes actions and performances which are to someone's *credit*; *credulous* generally refers to a person's character but 'gullible' or 'naive' do the same job.

D D D D D

DE FACTO *or* DE JURE

This pair of Latin phrases is usually found together, as balanced as a pair of scales, but they are opposites and shouldn't be confused.

De facto means 'in fact', 'actually', and applies to the situation that exists without regard to what is rightful or what the law says about it.

In contrast, *de jure* means 'by right', 'according to law'. So, in the example below, the writer states that Hitler and the rest were absolute rulers as a matter of fact and also because the laws of their respective countries said that they were:

> *For one thing, Hitler, Mussolini and Hirohito were all sovereign rulers, de jure as well as de facto.* (Daily Telegraph)

De facto is sometimes allowed out by itself. In the following example, the writer means that, whatever the libel laws say, in practice they do not operate:

> *In the US, there is virtually no legal protection for a public figure, especially a political one, from defamation. Libel laws are de facto defunct.* (Guardian)

Embarrassment rating: ●●● High if you get them the wrong way round, since any person who uses such 'specialist' terms should know better. In practice, it's probably the reader or listener who must pause for a moment to work out which definition belongs to which phrase.

How to avoid: *De facto* suggests the *fact*-based, actual state of affairs, while *de jure* echoes a set of other legal terms beginning 'jur-' ('jury', 'jurisdiction').

DEFECTIVE *or* DEFICIENT

There is a considerable overlap of meaning between these two but also a useful difference.

Defective means 'faulty', 'badly made', 'not working to full effect', and can apply to body parts ('defective genes') as well as gadgets or merchandise:

...my workstation as I now expect to find it – ie, with no chair, someone else's defective mouse and my phone facing the wrong way. (Observer)

Deficient means 'falling short', 'lacking in some way'. The word is not necessarily critical, or not as critical as *defective*. However, it usually implies that something could be better done:

From locker room to court house, the Rusedski saga has exposed the ATP's anti-doping procedures as deficient. (Guardian)

Embarrassment rating: ○○○ Nil to very low, since the terms are used almost interchangeably.

How to avoid: It's hard to pin down the difference here, but *defective* tends to apply to an item or faculty which was working properly and is now faulty, while *deficient* describes a shortage or lack of something which was never there in the first place. Thus eyesight which fails with age is *defective*, while a diet which is lacking in iron may be *deficient*.

DEFINITE *or* DEFINITIVE

It's tempting to use these words interchangeably although they carry quite distinct meanings: *definitive* is not simply a more emphatic form of *definite*.

Definite means 'exact', 'not vague':

Have you got any definite plans for the summer?

Definitive means 'decisive', 'final':

...he had excessively high hematocrit in his body – taken as a possible but not definitive indication of doping. (Independent)

Definitive also carries the sense of 'setting a standard':

His version of Macbeth *is likely to be the definitive one for a generation.*

Embarrassment rating: ●○○ Ambiguity results if the wrong word is used. There is a difference between a *definite* plan (i.e. a clear one) and a *definitive* one (i.e. one which can't be changed or improved on).

How to avoid: *Definitive* is one stage down the road from *definite*, and the first word should only be used when the sense of 'concluding' or 'absolute' is required.

DEPENDANT *or* DEPENDENT

The problem – or trick – with these two, one a noun, the other an adjective, comes in getting the ending right. Though spelled slightly differently they sound the same, hence the confusion. And the *independent* parallel is no help, since that word does not change according to what part of speech it is.

Dependant is a noun only and describes 'someone who depends on another for support' (usually financial):

She had four dependants, including her aged mother.

Dependent is an adjective meaning 'contingent', 'relying on':

The college place is dependent on his results.

It is incorrect to use the '-ant' spelling for this adjective:

They will inevitably become even more dependant [should be dependent] *on drug company influence.* (Private Eye)

(*Independent* has only one spelling whether it is used as a noun or an adjective: she stood as an *independent* in the election; an *independent* analysis.)

Embarrassment rating: ●○○ , because this is quite a frequent mistake and a forgivable one too. In any case, the meaning is not obscured.

How to avoid: *Dependant* and 'pendant' are both nouns. But in truth you either know this one or have to go to the dictionary each time. Sorry.

DIAGNOSIS *or* PROGNOSIS

This is one of those which-comes-first confusions. One word looks backwards, the other forwards.

Although *diagnosis* can be used more generally, the original meaning of the word refers to the 'identification of a medical condition through its symptoms':

The first thing that GPs learn about making a diagnosis is that bombarding the patient with closed questions is the worst way to go about it. (The Times)

The *prognosis* can only take place after the *diagnosis* since it is the 'forecast of the likely development' (of the disease or condition). Both words are often used outside a medical context, *diagnosis* to mean simply an 'analysis' and *prognosis* a 'prediction':

When a Thomas Hardy character says: 'You'll catch your death sitting there', you know it's not a figure of speech but a grave clinical prognosis. (Guardian)

Embarrassment rating: ●●○ But there is more than a shade of difference here. The question 'What's your diagnosis?' asks for a summary of a situation or problem so far, while the question 'What's your prognosis?' is a request for an informed prediction based on a *diagnosis*.

How to avoid: A *prognosis* is a projection forward into the future.

DISCREET *or* DISCRETE

These two words, originally derived from the same Latin word, are pronounced identically and also share the idea of 'keeping apart'. But they have acquired quite different meanings.

Discreet is used almost always in the sense of 'being able to keep secrets or confidences' and therefore 'careful or tactful':

Doctors are expected to be discreet in their treatment of patients.

This word shouldn't be confused with *discrete* which means 'separate' and tends to be applied to abstract rather than concrete things:

...it's hard to understand why psychiatrists still cling to the idea that madness and sanity are discrete. (Observer)

The frequent confusion between these two may be made worse by the fact that the noun from *discreet*, 'discretion', looks uncommonly as if it's derived from *discrete*.

Embarrassment rating: ●◑○ Any misunderstanding is likely to be for the reader who wonders whether *discrete* is a misprint for *discreet*, since there are contexts in which either word would make sense (e.g. 'a discrete approach to a problem'.)

How to avoid: *Discreet* is the more usual word and tends to be applied to people; *discrete* rather applies to ideas, categories, etc. and is found in more technical or impersonal contexts.

DRAFT *or* DRAUGHT

These words are very easily confused. They are pronounced the same, and both are connected to different senses of 'draw'.

Draft has the sense of 'something drawn'. As a noun it is a 'first version' of something like a plan or document, and as a verb it means to 'produce a rough, early version':

He drafted the outline of his speech on the back of an envelope.

This kind of *draft* involves words, and its producer would be a *draftsman* – this second sense and spelling is not often found.

By contrast, a *draughtsman* is 'someone who works with designs or pictures'. The word *draught* is more concerned with the 'act of drawing' and is the spelling used to describe 'beer which is drawn from the cask', or the 'current of air' which is drawn through a partly open door.

(US English, sensibly, has only one spelling: everything is draft. One of the American senses of *draft* is 'compel [someone] to do military service', the British equivalent being 'call up', although the use of the term has faded with the disappearance of National Service.)

Embarrassment rating: ●○○ Even if mistakes are made the meaning is usually clear, although to talk of *draft* beer would suggest a proposed beer which hadn't yet been brewed, while reference to a writer producing a first *draught* conjures up an odd image . . .

How to avoid: *Drafting* is only to do with words and plans: think of the 'f ' in fair copy. The current-of-air sense of draught might be remembered through their shared 'u'. And regular drinkers (also with a 'u') are likely to know their *draught* ales.

DUAL *or* DUEL

Two identically pronounced words which are quite easily confused, perhaps suggested by the idea of the 'two' sides involved in a *duel*.

Dual is an adjective meaning 'twofold': *dual* controls, a *dual* personality:
> *The briefcase, however, serves a dual purpose. It holds documents. But right now, as he walks towards me, it is also acting as a sort of fig leaf.*
> (The Times)

Duel is a noun or verb indicating an 'arranged fight between two individuals'. In the days of pistols-at-dawn, a *duel* would be fought over some abstract concern like honour or sometimes a woman. But in a less romantic age a *duel* is simply a 'contest between two sides'.

Embarrassment rating: ●●○ , since these words are part of everyday vocabulary and any mistake – as in an erroneous reference to 'duel carriageway' – looks like straightforward carelessness.

How to avoid: A *duel* is always connected to a quarrel of some kind and their shared endings will help in getting the spelling right.

E E E E E

ECONOMIC *or* ECONOMICAL

These two terms are frequently used as if they amounted to the same thing but there is a gap between their meanings.

Economic means 'relating to the economy', and can be used on several levels from the global or the national down to the personal:

> ...the Debtor Personality, which is essentially an unwillingness to allow your personal growth to be contained by mere economic constraints.
> (Daily Telegraph)

Economical is an altogether more homely term, and when applied to an individual means 'careful with money' (with a hint of stinginess); when used about products it suggests that the consumer is getting value for money:

> This is an economical car: it averages 50 mpg.

Economical can also suggest 'sparing', 'small in quantity' (an economical portion).

Embarrassment rating: ●◑○ *Economic* is often found where *economical* would be more accurate (as in, an *economic* car) and the sense is usually clear. But there would be potential confusion, for example, in a mistaken reference to an *economic/al* speech since the talk could either be about economics or simply be a brief one.

How to avoid: *Economic* is connected to *economics*, famously termed the 'dismal science' in the 19th century. *Economical* is related to the 'thrift' sense of *economy*, and like 'frugal' ends in 'al'.

ELECTRIC, ELECTRICAL *or* ELECTRIFYING

Only one of these words is usually applied in a literal sense, but which?

All these terms derive from 'electricity' but *electric* is used in a figurative sense to mean 'exciting' or 'startling' (an *electric* performance; an *electric* intervention in a debate) as well as in its literal application (*electric* light).

Electrical simply means 'related to electricity' and is applied to supplies, faults, etc. (an *electrical* breakdown). The adjective *electrifying* is almost always used in the figurative sense of *electric* but carries an even stronger charge: 'astonishing'.

Embarrassment rating: ●●○○, if a careless choice of word leaves the sense uncertain. An *electric* interruption could be taken to mean an exciting break or intervention in proceedings, while an *electrical* interruption would always describe a period when the power is off.

How to avoid: If you intend to refer to supplies of electricity, use *electrical*. When describing events, atmospheres, etc. the other two words are appropriate.

EMOTIONAL *or* EMOTIVE

Both words are obviously connected to *emotion*, but have different applications.

Emotional tends to be used in the sense of 'excitable' or 'moody'. The word sometimes has a slightly critical edge to it. Years ago *Private Eye* adopted the phrase 'tired and emotional' for 'drunk' to avoid being sued by Members of Parliament and others. But *emotional* primarily means 'related to the emotions' (as opposed to the head), as here:

Love, on the other hand, strikes me as the emotional equivalent of hollandaise sauce. (The Times)

Emotive means 'intended to stir the emotions'. It's usually applied to language and sometimes to images which set out to manipulate an audience by triggering certain responses:

The highly emotive advertisement suggested that the Massachusetts Governor was so soft on criminals that he happily released such men from jail. (The Times)

Embarrassment rating: ●●○○, since an *emotional* speech is not the same as an *emotive* one. But my feeling is that both of these adjectives are slightly tainted. *Emotional*, rarely used in a neutral, descriptive sense, carries a dismissive note as in 'an emotional person'. And to characterise anything as *emotive* is to suggest that you are aware of, and probably resent, some attempt at manipulation.

How to avoid: *Emotive* cannot be used of people, but only of words and images, topics, subjects, and so on.

EMPATHY *or* SYMPATHY

Both nouns are to do with feeling, and probably because they describe somewhat amorphous reactions tend to blur into each other. However, they have fairly different applications which are worth preserving.

Empathy is 'imaginative identification with someone else' and his or her situation, whether that situation is a good or bad one:

He [John Edwards] has shown a real flair for the 'I feel your pain' empathy that Bill Clinton made his own. (The Times)

Sympathy also involves the attempt to see things from the perspective of another person and carries the additional sense of 'compassion':

As we'd only recently been burgled ourselves I had sympathy for the neighbours when their house was broken into.

(The related verbs are empathise and sympathise.)

Embarrassment rating: OOO It's generally seen as a good thing to show either empathy or sympathy, and the person on the receiving end probably won't be quibbling over which it is.

How to avoid: *Sympathy* is the more familiar and somehow the 'warmer' term – tea and sympathy, anyone? – while *empathy* seems less spontaneous. Indeed, much education and training now involves 'empathy exercises', suggesting a slightly artificial quality to the feeling.

EMULATE *or* IMITATE

Both of these terms are to do with 'copying' and are sometimes used interchangeably. But their associations are quite different and worth noting.

To *emulate* is to 'imitate' but it carries more positive overtones than the second word because the idea of rivalry is often involved rather than mere copying. Therefore to *emulate* is also to 'try to equal or outdo'. However, in the example below, *imitate* might have been more accurate since it refers to viewers' home-grown attempts to perform hospital-style operations:

Medical organisations believe there could be merit in television operations but there are concerns that viewers might emulate [?should be imitate] procedures, as has occurred with drama series such as Casualty. (The Times)

To *imitate* is simply to 'copy'. The word frequently has negative associations – imitations are much more often described as poor than good.

Embarrassment rating: ●◑O, since one term is generally complimentary while the other is not. Unless one is talking about deliberate mimicry, to suggest that someone is *imitating* another person in behaviour, achievements, etc. is not to praise them. But to *emulate* has more of a follow-in-the-footsteps-of sense to it and doesn't imply the loss of personality which is involved in imitation.

How to avoid: *Emulate* should be reserved for positive, approving contexts.

ENDEMIC, EPIDEMIC *or* PANDEMIC

Three terms which are widely linked to outbreaks (of disease) and their spread. The differences between them are sometimes blurred.

Endemic, an adjective, means 'widely found among a certain group or in a certain area', and although often referring to disease it can extend to other topics:

Poverty and prostitution were endemic in Victorian London.

Epidemic is a noun or adjective describing an 'outbreak' – usually of a disease (though one could talk of 'an e*pidemic* of panic'). A characteristic of an *epidemic* is that it is relatively short-lived, unlike something *endemic*, which is likely to be there for good:

The school was hit by an epidemic of flu after Christmas.

Pandemic (noun and adjective) is an *epidemic* on a grand scale; something 'affecting a whole people', even on a global scale:

Keeping up with the Joneses has been thoroughly rebranded as Status Anxiety – a vast pandemic that afflicts the entire civilised world. (Daily Telegraph)

Embarrassment rating: ●●○ To refer to a condition as *endemic* when *epidemic* is meant, or vice versa, could cause confusion.

How to avoid: Something which is *endemic* has to be *endured*, since it is a localised, long-lasting condition or illness which is very difficult to eradicate. By contrast, an *epidemic* strikes suddenly.

ENORMITY *or* ENORMOUSNESS

Two words both deriving from *enormous* and suggesting size, although the principal meaning of the first word is connected to crimes of great magnitude. (The Latin root of *enormous* indicates something which has deviated from the rule or norm.)

The first word in this pair is definitely the more widely used of the two, whatever the context. Strictly speaking, there is a distinction, since the noun *enormity* characterises 'extreme wickedness' or an 'outrage':

...the enormity of Hitler's crimes had been exposed... (The Times)

In recent years the word has also been employed in the sense of 'vastness' (i.e. *enormousness*), although quite a lot of people dislike the usage. This sense, relating purely to size, may eventually push out the original meaning of 'outrage', and then we shall be one word poorer. For the moment, though, there's something odd about a phrase like this:

The enormity of the universe... (Guardian)

Here the first response of some readers could be to wonder what crime the universe has committed.

The preference for *enormity*, when what is really meant is *enormousness*, may have something to do with the slightly cumbersome quality of the longer word, and there are contexts when the two senses do seem to blur together:

Yossarian choked on his toast and eggs at the enormity of his error...
(*Joseph Heller*, Catch-22)

Embarrassment rating: ●○○ , because *enormity* is so frequently used to describe something of great size (and there is some dictionary support for this sense).

How to avoid: Careful users will still want to differentiate between the two words. The link between *enormity* and criminality may be helpful, while the lumbering length of *enormousness* seems to hint at the meaning of that word.

EQUABLE *or* EQUITABLE

Both of these adjectives contain ideas of balance and evenness, but they are found in different areas.

The adjective *equable* means 'even', 'without extremes'. Frequently applied to the weather, where it means much the same as 'temperate', it also describes character:

He had such an equable temperament that it was impossible to pick a quarrel or an argument with him.

Equitable means 'just', 'following the principles of fairness':

Last year Kenya called for the treaty to be revised, but all efforts to negotiate a more equitable arrangement have failed. (The Times)

Embarrassment rating: ●●○ It would be an error, for example, to talk about an 'equitable climate'.

How to avoid: *Equable* is used only of individuals (and the weather); like 'peaceable', 'tractable', and 'biddable', all descriptions of easygoing people, it has three syllables. The longer word *equitable* is more abstract and applies to decisions, judgements and arrangements.

ESCAPEE, ESCAPER, ESCAPIST or ESCAPOLOGIST

The four words characterise the individual who seeks to get out of somewhere uncomfortable or confining, but each of them crops up in a different context.

An *escapee* is 'one who escapes'. The word almost always has a literal application to describe the person who gets out of a jail, a POW camp and so on. An alternative form is *escaper*.

An *escapist* is a 'person who is looking to escape from reality'. This word – most usually found as an adjective describing books, films and so on – doesn't necessarily carry a negative charge. But someone who gravitates towards escapist material all the time may not be in a healthy state of mind:

> *...he argues that the flood of books about fairies and angels and Incas and crystals is a symptom of escapist despair by people who feel impotent to improve their lives...* (Guardian)

An *escapologist* is a 'person who repeatedly gets out of tricky situations'. Originally used about those showmen and magicians who made their living out of escaping from 'impossible' situations (involving chains, padlocks, barrels flung into rivers, and the rest), it's now applied to politicians and, well, politicians:

> *Let us be in no doubt: last week belonged to the prime minister. The great escapologist has wriggled out again.* (Sunday Telegraph)

(The related abstract nouns are *escapism* and *escapology*.)

Embarrassment rating: ●○○, since these terms carry distinct meanings. *Escapist* reading is quite different from *escapologist* reading (if such a genre exists).

How to avoid: The straightforward *escapee* will do for one who gets out of physical confinement. The *escapist* may be confined in some sense as well, but his or her escape will be inwards to the realms of fantasy. The -ology/-ologist endings to *escapology/escapologist* indicate that this is a kind of profession or a field of study.

EVIDENCE or EVINCE

Two similar-sounding words which involve ideas of displaying or proving.

Evidence is mainly found in its noun use (the *evidence* in the case) but it can also be used as a verb with the sense of to 'make evident', to 'show':

> *It had been a poor year for the company, as evidenced by the figures.*

Some people don't like – all right, I don't like – this verb use of *evidence*. It sounds awkward and a simple word like 'show' will do a better job.

Evince means to 'show clearly', and is used of people rather than figures, data, etc.:

He never evinced much interest in investment or business transactions... (The Times)

Embarrassment rating: OOO , although substituting *evidence* for *evince*, as in 'He never evidenced much interest...', sounds cumbersome.

How to avoid: More straightforward terms such as 'demonstrate' or 'show' are often preferable to these two terms.

EXHAUSTED, EXHAUSTING *or* EXHAUSTIVE

Because of its shared root in the verb *exhaust*, the third of these terms is sometimes confused with the second one.

Exhausted is simply 'very tired':

Working for six months without a break left her totally exhausted.

Exhausting means 'very tiring':

She found it exhausting to go for so long without a holiday.

Exhaustive means 'very thorough':

When she came back she gave us an exhaustive account of her holidays.

Embarrassment rating: ●◑O There is a faint connection between *exhaustive* and *exhausting*, in that a study, discussion, etc. which is *exhaustive* may also be *exhausting* for the participants. For this reason it's necessary to be clear about which word to use.

How to avoid: *Exhausted* applies principally to living things (although one can talk of supplies, etc. being *exhausted*, i.e. used up). *Exhausting* describes the experience which has caused exhaustion. *Exhaustive* tends to be used of abstract things such as investigations, lists and inquiries: like 'comprehensive', another word meaning all-inclusive, it ends in '–ive'.

EXTEMPORE *or* IMPROMPTU

Two words from Latin which are frequently used interchangeably although there are subtle differences of emphasis and application between them.

Extempore describes a speech, performance, etc. which is done 'off the cuff', 'without the help of notes' but not necessarily without any preparation:

...she [Mary Queen of Scots] had given an extempore Latin oration in the Louvre at the age of 13 on the education of women... (Daily Telegraph)

Impromptu also applies to performances with the sense of 'unprepared', but it carries the additional meaning of 'makeshift' and can describe arrangements, structures and so on:

Around the city impromptu car dealerships have sprung up on roadsides offering everything from old bangers to second-hand BMWs. (Guardian)

Embarrassment rating: ●○○ In most contexts involving speech or performance the two terms can be swapped around. But it would be incorrect to use *extempore* in the *Guardian* quote above.

How to avoid: *Impromptu* will generally do, but if you mean to imply that the speaker or performer knew what was coming – as Mary Queen of Scots surely did (see first quote) – then use *extempore*.

F F F F F

FAIR or FARE

The biggest traps sometimes lie in the simplest words. This is a pair of confusables, like 'bail/bale', with a raft of meanings attached.

Fair as a noun describes a 'market for business or pleasure'(antiques *fair*, trade *fair*, fun*fair*). As an adjective, *fair* has a range of meanings from 'bright' (a fair day) to 'just' (a fair exchange) to the very English 'not bad' (*fair* marks). As a verb *fare* means to 'travel' or 'get on' – not much found now except in slightly quaint expressions like 'How are you faring?' As a noun a *fare* is the 'price of a journey' (train *fare*) or 'food/provisions', although this second sense seems restricted to supermarket advertising and the hospitality industry. Only a local hostelry actually talks about putting *fare* on the table, as in *The farm also offers a tea room with traditional fare...*

Embarrassment rating: ●○○ Any mistake will emerge only in writing and the meaning is unlikely to be affected.

How to avoid: Except when it carries the noun sense of 'market', *fair* is an adjective, and so will always be found describing something or somebody. By contrast, *fare* usually occurs in its noun form (bus *fare*) and so can stand alone.

FANCIFUL, IMAGINARY or IMAGINATIVE

Three words associated with the imagination but with widely differing meanings.

'Fancy' in its old sense is connected to the 'imagination', since it was regarded as a kind of younger brother, a bit wilder and more frivolous. This historical sense has pretty well disappeared but the adjective *fanciful* occupies ground somewhere between imaginative and silly; best defined perhaps as 'unrealistic':

> But it would be fanciful to claim that [the Lottery] has to compete with betting shops or casinos, whose customers are rather different.
> (Daily Telegraph)

Imaginary means 'having no basis in reality', 'illusory':

Middle Earth was Tolkien's imaginary landscape in Lord of the Rings.

Imaginative means 'showing imagination' in a creative sense:

Using only a couple of chairs the group staged an imaginative reconstruction of the trial.

Embarrassment rating: ●●●, if the second and third are confused, something which is quite easy to do. There is a large gap between characterising someone as *imaginative* (i.e. having an active imagination – not always a compliment) and calling them *imaginary* (which would imply that they don't exist). The word *fanciful*, whether applied to people or to ideas, is usually pejorative.

How to avoid: There's no short cut to memory here. Simply take care over which word is meant.

FEMININE, EFFEMINATE *or* EFFETE

Almost everyone is aware of the difference between the first two words, but many assume mistakenly that *effete* – probably because of the similarity of sound and the contexts in which the word often appears – means the same as *effeminate*.

Feminine means 'characteristic of women' and although used principally of women (obviously!) it can describe an attribute which a man might have: a *feminine* voice; a *feminine* sensitivity. *Effeminate*, only used of men, means 'woman-like' and so 'unmanly' – it's a pejorative term:

Today, he can hold forth about bedtime stories and potty training without the risk of being thought effeminate. (Daily Telegraph)

Effete has nothing to do with *effeminate* but, by a rather complicated process, moves from meaning 'worn out' (originally through childbirth) to 'barren' to 'degenerate'. In fact, the usual application of the word is lighter than its serious history suggests and *effete* winds up meaning something between 'useless' and 'frivolous':

And there is something pleasingly effete about the existence of three artisan chocolate-makers within a few hundred metres of each other. (The Times)

Embarrassment rating: ●○○ To be described as *effete* is often disparaging (although not in the example above) but it is nowhere near as insulting as *effeminate*. Even if *effete* packs less of a punch than it appears to, you may still be misunderstood.

How to avoid: Of these three words, only *feminine* is a word of unqualified approval – and that in particular contexts. The other two need careful handling.

FEWER or LESS

These words are frequently swapped for each other in speech and writing but formal English makes a distinction between them.

Both of these adjectival comparatives (*few/fewer; little/less*) indicate a smaller number or quantity. *Fewer* should be used when referring to a number of objects or people (i.e. with a plural noun):

There were fewer swimmers in the pool today.

Less should be applied to any singular item or unit:

Diet experts advise us to put less salt on our food.

Not many people would think to use *fewer* in the above sentence but it is quite common to find the mistake made the other way round, that is, *less* employed with plural nouns:

There are less openings for graduates in this area.

Not only is *fewer openings* grammatically correct but it sounds better as well.

Embarrassment rating: ●○○ As indicated above, this tends to be a one-way mistake, with *less* being erroneously put for *fewer*.

How to avoid: *Fewer* indicates a smaller number, *less* a smaller amount, so it helps to step back one degree from the comparative and substitute *few* and *little* in the original sentence: you can say *few* openings but not *little* openings, and *little* salt but not *few* salt.

FLOTSAM or JETSAM

These two generally appear together, but there is a small difference in their original sea-going definitions even though the product ends up in the same place. So it is one of those 'which-way-round-is-it?' differences.

Flotsam describes 'any items lost during a shipwreck and later found floating in the water'. *Jetsam* applies to 'items which are deliberately thrown overboard' (e.g. to lighten the ship). The pair almost always have a metaphorical application now. *Flotsam* quite often appears by itself, sometimes with a glance at its nautical roots:

...the American public and much of the rest of the world believed that after Saddam's regime sank, a vast flotsam of weapons of mass destruction would bob to the surface. (Guardian)

but *jetsam* is almost invariably coupled with *flotsam*:

...her own office is free of any of the flotsam and jetsam that bogs down mere mortals. (Guardian)

Embarrassment rating: ○○○, imagine, unless you're talking to a literal-minded sea dog or an amateur yachtsperson.

How to avoid: *Flotsam* is what is found floating in the water; *jetsam* is what has been intentionally ejected overboard.

FORBEAR *or* FOREBEAR

Two words not always distinct in their spelling but with no connection in meaning.

To *forbear* (with the stress falling on the second syllable) is to 'abstain', to 'hold back from'. The word is really for formal use, especially in its past tense form of *forbore*:

He was severely criticised in the report but forbore from making a public response.

A *forebear* (which can also be spelled *forbear* but with the stress falling on the first syllable, regardless of spelling) is an 'ancestor', usually from several generations back.

If the Greeks are guilty of anything, it is hubris, a failing their classical forebears identified and gave its name. (Guardian)

Embarrassment rating: ●○○ The words are different parts of speech – *forbear* a verb, *forebear* a noun – so mistakes over meaning are unlikely.
How to avoid: Your *forebears* are those who have gone be*fore* you. But the *forbear* spelling will always be correct, whichever word you are using.

FORCEFUL, FORCIBLE *or* FORCED

Like many sets of adjectives which derive from a single noun, in this case *force*, the meanings of the individual words carry distinct shades of meaning.

Forceful, meaning 'with force' or 'vigorous', tends to be used about a person's character, attitude or words:

[He] was a man of forceful personality and strong opinions. (Daily Telegraph)
Forcible can also be found in this sense of 'imposing' (a *forceful/forcible* speaker), but it more usually has a physical context and means 'employing force' – one step away from 'violent':

The police made a forcible removal of the demonstrators from the scene.
Forced has a variety of meanings from 'strained' (a *forced* smile) to 'rapidly ripened' (*forced* fruit) and 'compelled' (*forced* removal).

Embarrassment rating: ●○○, since *forceful* and *forcible* are often interchangeable. But not always. There is a difference between, say, a *forceful* entry, which would be one that impressed spectators, and a *forcible* entry, which would probably do some damage to the door.
How to avoid: *Forceful* is more to do with manner; *forcible* and, sometimes, *forced* carry the suggestion of physical coercion.

FOREGO *or* FORGO

As with a number of word pairs beginning 'for-/fore-', it is easy to get confused over which form to use.

To *forego* is to 'go in front of'. It is hardly ever – or never? – used except in the forms of *foregoing* and *foregone* (the *foregoing* points in an argument, a *foregone* conclusion).

To *forgo*, which has the alternative spelling *forego*, is to 'do without something':

When his parents were away, he was obliged to forego his usual tasty Tuscan food for the cooking of an English aunt... (Guardian)

Embarrassment rating: ●○○ Even though it would be incorrect to refer to, say, a 'forgone conclusion', the meaning remains clear. The error would probably pass unnoticed.

How to avoid: The *foregone/foregoing* spelling can be remembered by splitting it into its component parts: going be*fore*.

FORTUITOUS *or* FORTUNATE

Fortuitous has gradually been encroaching on the territory of fortunate, and it is frequently used in the sense of the second word although its primary meaning is different.

Strictly speaking, *fortuitous* means 'occurring by chance':

They were just talking about him when he made a fortuitous appearance at the door.

while *fortunate* is 'lucky':

Given the nature of her offence, she was fortunate to receive only a suspended sentence.

But the similarity between the two words means that *fortuitous* is generally used to suggest an element of (good) luck combined with chance:

The timing of the Beatles' arrival [in America] in February 1964 was fortuitous. Coming just three months after the assassination of President Kennedy, their melodic songs and youthful optimism offered relief to a nation cast in deep gloom. (The Times)

Embarrassment rating: ●○○, since this application of **fortuitous** is so well dug in that it is close to standard use. This is fine as long as the listener or reader is on the same wavelength as the user; if they're not, there is potential confusion in a statement like 'Her arrival was fortuitous'. (Was it by chance or was it lucky?)

How to avoid: *Fortunate* is straightforward, but if you really mean that some event is accidental (rather than lucky) then it may be safer to avoid *fortuitous* altogether in favour of 'by chance' or 'accidental'. Note that people can be described as *fortunate* while events, arrivals, etc. are *fortuitous*.

FULSOME *or* HEARTFELT

These two are near opposites, yet the first word is sometimes used as if it meant the same as the second. It doesn't.

Fulsome is a tricky word to interpret because it often occurs in an ambiguous context. Meaning 'sickeningly admiring', it suggests hypocrisy, smarminess, as here:

Whatever fulsome reassurances about BBC independence drop from the lips of Tony Blair, Tessa Jowell, Alastair Campbell... (Observer)

But when *fulsome* is applied to, say, 'praise' or 'apology', it's not always clear whether the writer intends it in the (mistaken) sense of *abundant*, probably suggested by the 'ful-' prefix. If you want to convey sincerity then *heartfelt* is a better word, as it means what it says, i.e. 'deeply felt':

And when he claimed that Tory opposition to the bill was 'principled', Labour MPs at last had an excuse for heartfelt, scornful, pipe-clearing laughter. (Guardian)

Embarrassment rating: ●●○ To talk, say, of *fulsome* praise is not really complimentary, although it is sometimes taken to be.

How to avoid: '*Fulsome* apology' and '*fulsome* praise' are virtually clichés nowadays. That said, it's occasionally better to choose another word altogether rather than risk being misunderstood. Hence, 'insincere' or 'superficial' may be preferable to *fulsome*.

G G G G G

GAMBIT, GAMUT *or* GAUNTLET

These terms are sometimes confused, the first and second probably on account of their similar sound and specialised uses and the second and third because they are often associated with the word 'run'.

A *gambit* is an 'opening move', originally in chess (where the term applied to the deliberate sacrifice of a piece to gain an advantage).

Now the term is extended to any 'thought-out manoeuvre which begins a game, negotiation, etc:

The team's intimidating gambit was to utter a series of war cries before each match.

(Incidentally, to talk about an *opening gambit* is a redundant repetition – all *gambits* are opening ones, by definition.)

Gamut means 'range', 'the full spectrum':

Sir Edwin Lutyens's fluent drawings run the full gamut, from monumental projects to cosy, intimate spaces. (Independent)

The first word is quite often found, incorrectly, where the second is meant:

*' ...a whole range of things, a whole gambit [should be **gamut**] of ideas...'* (Radio 4)

A *gauntlet* was originally an 'armoured glove', something thrown down by a knight as a formal challenge. Confusingly, in the familiar phrase 'run the gauntlet' – meaning to 'undergo a punishing process' – the *gauntlet* has nothing to do with a glove but is a mangled derivation from a Swedish word describing a course down a path! Whatever the source of the term, the phrase 'run the gamut' is absolutely distinct from 'run the gauntlet'.

Embarrassment rating: ●●◐, since different meanings are conveyed by each word.

How to avoid: A *gambit* is the first move in a *game* which may be *bitterly* contested. A *gamut* describes a full spectrum – note the shared 'u's.

GOURMAND or GOURMET

As with those other French terms also connected with good living, 'bon vivant' and 'bon viveur' (see earlier entry), there is widespread uncertainty over the distinction between a *gourmand* and a *gourmet*.

Being called a *gourmand* is not a compliment since it means a 'glutton', a greedy eater who doesn't mind what goes down as long as he/she gets enough of it. What the writer of the following sentence presumably meant was *gourmet*, since a straightforward *gourmand* wouldn't be much use for the Michelin guide:

> He was also something of a gourmand [?should be **gourmet**] and once confessed that if he had to pick another career it would be as a food critic for the Michelin Restaurant guide. (Daily Telegraph)

A *gourmet* is a 'person with refined tastes in food and drink'. The word is also an adjective meaning 'refined', as here:

> Most cookbooks now cater for after-work foodies who want to produce a gourmet meal in 30 minutes flat. (Daily Telegraph)

Embarrassment rating: ●●○ , if you use *gourmand* in place of *gourmet* and if the reader's or listener's French is better than yours. Of course you may actually intend to say *gourmand* . . .

How to avoid: ...but if you actually mean *gourmand*, then why not say 'glutton' and avoid ambiguity? *Gourmet* should be reserved for those people or dining experiences that deserve it. Like other words denoting quality – 'classic' springs to mind – it has become devalued through indiscriminate application.

GRAND or GRANDIOSE

These two look alike but more separates them than unites them.

The difference between the adjectives is that *grand* should be applied to something which is authentically 'splendid', while *grandiose* suggests that what is described is somehow 'inflated' or 'false'. A *grand* building is large and very imposing, a *grand* scheme is ambitious and conceived on a great scale. *Grandiose* ideas, by contrast, are hollow; they sound good but will never amount to anything.

(*Grand* also has some currency as a colloquial term of approval, like 'brilliant', 'great', etc., although the term is dated now.)

Embarrassment rating: ●●◑ , since to term something *grandiose* is to imply criticism while to call it *grand* is usually a straightforward compliment.

How to avoid: Anything which is *grandiose* has something false about it.

HANGED *or* HUNG

These are the past tense forms of the verb to *hang*. There's a tendency to use *hung* for everything and everybody. *Hanged* should be used in one context, however.

In general things should be *hung*. Pictures on walls, coats on racks, meat in the butcher's; *hung* can apply even to people when they are clinging on to something:

He hung from the window sill by his fingertips.

The single exception is in the context of capital punishment, when the individual is *hanged*. The wrong form of the word is often used:

He was arrested immediately, found guilty of 'moral insanity' and hung [should be *hanged*]. (Big Issue)

Embarrassment rating: ●◐○ This is a common error but correct usage demands that a person who is executed with a noose is *hanged*.

How to avoid: The profession of hangman, now fortunately gone, or the old game of 'hangman' indicates the right version of the word when you are referring to the ultimate punishment, i.e. *hanged*.

HEROIN or HEROINE

That final 'e' makes all the difference, and the slip is easily made (see below).

Heroin is the 'drug which is a morphine derivative', while *heroine* is the female equivalent of 'hero', a 'woman who shows heroic qualities' or the 'central woman character either in real life or in a story, film, etc.' (e.g. Jane Eyre, Cleopatra). Although there's a tendency now to use a single term to apply to both men and women in some artistic contexts – actor, poet – the hero/heroine distinction tends to be observed. It is even more important to preserve the heroin/heroine difference:

Charles Saatchi has angered the parents of a dead heroine [should be **heroin**] *addict by buying and exhibiting a macabre portrait of her...* (The Times)

Embarrassment rating: ●●●, because the mistake looks like carelessness, which it is.

How to avoid: Just be on the alert. It might help to recall that '-ine' is the ending of 'feminine' as well as *heroine*.

HOARD *or* HORDE

These two have the same sound and share overlapping ideas of mass and quantity.

A *hoard* is a 'hidden store' of something, usually valuable and put by for use in the future:

Rumours of a hoard of Nazi treasure at the bottom of the lake circulated for many years.

Horde describes a 'large number':

There were hordes of people in Oxford Street for the sales.

The first word is wrongly used here instead of the second:

...someone who can fight the hungry hoards [should be *hordes*] *of other people who are going to apply for this job!* (recruitment advertisement)

Embarrassment rating: ●○○ It is quite tricky to discriminate between these two and there's nothing in the 'shape' of either word to give guidance.

How to avoid: *Hoard* is frequently associated with treasure, and the words share an 'a'. *Hordes* tend to be fairly *horrible* too.

IMPLY *or* INFER

This is a very familiar pair of confusables. People – or at least those who care – have long complained about the misuse of *infer* to mean *imply*.

Properly used, these verbs have a complementary quality. To *imply* something is to 'hint' or 'suggest' it without its being openly stated:

> *The remuneration committee was still looking at this issue, the company said, implying that a severance pay-off has not been ruled out.* (Guardian)

To *infer* is to 'draw conclusions from the evidence', and suggests skill at understanding hints and working out implications:

> *The 21 Grams of the [film] title... is apparently the weight a body loses when it dies, from which we might infer it is the precise weight of the human soul.* (Guardian)

In this way one person will *infer* what another has *implied*, or (in noun terms) *inferences* will be drawn from *implications*.

Infer is sometimes used as though it meant *imply* – as in the erroneous 'I don't like your tone of voice. What are you inferring?' This usage gets some dictionary support, but it is wrong by the standards of correct English.

Embarrassment rating: ●◐○ As I've said, this is a pretty common error and sheer weight of numbers may eventually result in *infer* being used only in its wrong sense (rather as with 'disinterested/uninterested'). However, this is a distinction worth defending because, when used properly, *infer* is a useful and natural opposite to *imply*.

How to avoid: This is a hard distinction to memorise. How about: when you *infer* something you take *in* information; when you *imply* something, you send it *out*.

INNOVATION *or* INVENTION

These two are closely connected but in no way mean the same thing.

An *innovation* is the 'introduction of something fresh' – not as radical as an *invention*, it's usually the development or refinement of an existing idea or system:

> *CCTV coverage is extensive, but the real innovations are the movement sensors under each [car] bay.* (Guardian)

By contrast, an *invention* is a 'new device or discovery':

> *Marconi is generally credited with the invention of wireless telegraphy.*

Invention is also used in the sense of fiction – a 'deceit or lie'.

Embarrassment rating: ●○○ But historical accuracy demands that some people are credited with *inventions*, others with *innovations*, even if the distinction is often blurred.

How to avoid: *Invention* derives from a Latin root which means to 'come upon' – as if the discovery was lying hidden until the right person came along. To *innovate*, by contrast, has more to do with 'making new'; the idea of 'novel' and 'novelty' underlie it and share the same root. Like renovation, it describes an improvement to an existing system.

INNUENDO *or* INSINUATION

Both words describe something not openly stated but implied, and both have tacky associations.

An *innuendo* is an 'indirect remark', very frequently one with sexual overtones – it's often the equivalent of the French phrase 'double entendre', any remark with a nudge-nudge component:

> *The message is, 'In football girls really are on top' – those last two words picked out in pink, wink, wink. No sexual innuendo intended, says the FA.* (Guardian)

An *insinuation* is more general, being any 'hint carrying an unpleasant suggestion':

> *Mr Norman's comments about being better off ditching the vinaigrette and using Hellman's... amounted to an insinuation that his restaurant was buying in ready-made mayonnaise.* (Daily Telegraph)

(To *insinuate* is to 'hint' but also to 'work (oneself) gradually into a place' – an organisation, a person's good books – by stealth.)

Embarrassment rating: ●○○ Both words have slightly unpleasant connotations, and to make *innuendos* (plural also *innuendoes*) is probably on a par with making *insinuations*.

How to avoid: Insinuation will do for any indirect remark that aims to undermine another's reputation for honesty. *Innuendo* is generally found in a sexual context.

ITS *or* IT'S

This is one of the commonest and most basic mistakes in written English. It's the apostrophe which causes the problem, of course.

It's is the contracted or shortened form of *it is* or *it has*:

> *It's a warm day.*

> *It's been raining all day.*

Its, without an apostrophe, is the possessive form of the pronoun it:

> *The cat flicked its tail.*

Here is a selection of mistakes, going both ways. The following should read *its*, with no apostrophe:

> *...unlike common-or-garden spring mattresses which will sag with age latex will hold it's* [should be *its*] *shape...* (advertisement)

> *Unlike other films on this event, Kasdan and Costner's gives the gunfight it's* [should be *its*] *factual 30 seconds.* (Independent)

Getting it wrong the other way round (i.e. leaving out the apostrophe when it ought to be included) may be less usual but the mistake is still found too often:

> *...Arnold Schwarzenegger finds his memory has been erased – so its* [should be it's] *off to Mars in the hope of piecing together his past.* (Independent)

> *Staff without windows say they do not know whether its* [should be it's] *dark outside, if its* [should be it's] *raining, sunny, hot or cold...* (Sun)

But, just to show that it is possible to do it properly, the following example gets both spellings right in the right places:

> *But to its followers, it's the old story of demonising black subculture before exploiting its commercial fallout.* (Guardian)

Embarrassment rating: ●●● This may be a very frequent error but that does not make it any more excusable. It's easy enough to find the correct form (see below), and the failure to get it right indicates a poor grasp of the basics of written English.

How to avoid: If uncertain over which form to use – whether *it's* or *its* – try substituting the full-length *it is* or *it has* in the sentence. As long as the phrase or sentence still makes sense (*It is* a warm day; *It has* been raining all day), then you can safely use the contracted form of the two words (*It's* ..). If, however, the sentence does *not* make sense (the cat flicked *it is* tail), then you are using the possessive form of *it* and must not include the apostrophe: write *its*.

J J J J J J J

JUNCTION *or* JUNCTURE

Both words mean a 'joining or union' but occur in different contexts.

Junction tends to have a physical application, describing the point where roads or railway lines or electric wires meet. *Juncture* is a coming together in time rather than space, and suggests a 'critical point' in some process:

> *At that juncture Townsend and Princess Margaret were able to announce their love to each other – but not to the world.* (The Times)

Embarrassment rating: ●●○ The words don't sound right if swapped around. To put *junction* in the *Times* sentence above would suggest a royal version of the famous love-in-a-railway-station film *Brief Encounter*. Conversely, one can't talk of an electric *juncture*.

How to avoid: The *junction* association with trains, electricity, etc. is familiar to everyone. If the sentence is about time, rather than place, then *juncture* can be used. The term shouldn't be applied to just any old event – where a simple 'now' or 'then' would do – but be reserved for a significant moment.

K K K K K

KNELL or KNOLL

This isn't much of a trap perhaps but it may sometimes be assumed that *knoll* is the past tense form of *knell* (possibly under the influence of a bell *tol*ling). It isn't. Read on for enlightenment.

A *knell* describes the 'sound of a tolling bell' – particularly at a funeral. In fact the word is almost always used figuratively and prefaced with 'death':

> Days after the United States said it would scrap the space shuttle, the death knell has been sounded for the Hubble space telescope. (Daily Telegraph)

The verb is also *knell* (past tense *knelled*).

A *knoll* is a 'small hill'. I'd take a small bet that at least one in every four uses of this fairly uncommon word is in the phrase 'grassy knoll' – a reference to the roadside area in Dallas from where a gunman (other than Lee Harvey Oswald) is supposed by conspiracy buffs to have taken a shot at President Kennedy.

Embarrassment rating: ●○○ Most mistakes here are probably to do with correct spelling of *knell/knoll* rather than confusion over meanings.

How to avoid: *Knell* goes with be*ll*. *Knoll* goes with hil*l*ock.

LLLLLL

LAMA or LLAMA

It is surely the exotic source of these words – one from Tibetan, the other from Spanish via a Peruvian language – that sometimes causes confusion. There is nothing in them to hint at the meaning and so guide the spelling.

The *lama* with one 'l' is a 'Buddhist monk in Tibet':

> *Readers of* Cosmopolitan *who seek the serenity of a Buddhist lama but can't be fagged to put in hours of meditation each day for years can expect to be disappointed.* (Daily Telegraph)

The *llama* with two 'l's is a 'four-legged beast of burden', the South American equivalent of the camel (in fact camels and llamas are related):

> *It's not often that you're offered a dried llama foetus – unless you're in La Paz, that is.* (Daily Telegraph)

Don't confuse the man with the animal – for one thing, they come from opposite sides of the world:

> *They get a pleasant glow from name-dropping the Dalai Llama* [should be *Lama*]. (Daily Telegraph)

Embarrassment rating: ●◑○ People will know what you mean even if they detect the mistake. Amusing rather than embarrassing.

How to avoid: *Lama* and 'monk' have the same number of letters. So do the *llama* and the 'camel', its distant relation. Alternatively, both *llama* and 'woolly' have a double 'l'.

LATITUDE or LONGITUDE

This is one of those 'which-way-round-is-it?' confusions. Everyone is familiar with these imaginary lines which parcel up the globe, but which one runs from side to side and which from pole to pole?

Latitude is the 'angular distance from the equator, measured to the north or south' (so that Wellington, New Zealand is 41.17 degrees South while Wellington in Somerset, England is 50.59 degrees North). *Latitude* has the additional meanings of 'range' or 'freedom'.

Longitude uses the meridian, any one of the great and imaginary circles running from pole to pole, with the meridian line through Greenwich taken as the starting point. *Longitude* is therefore the 'angular distance between a particular place and the Greenwich meridian, measured to the east and west'. (Paris, Texas is 95.33 degrees West while Paris, France is 2.20 degrees East.)

Embarrassment rating: ●●○○, except for geography teachers or those who like messing about in boats – and presumably they already know the difference.

How to avoid: Lines of *longitude* run from pole to pole, and the two words contain an 'o' as the second letter. Getting this one right automatically defines *latitude*.

LAY *or* LIE

There aren't that many English confusables which one can honestly claim as nightmarish, but this is one of them. Not only do these basic words relate to the same sort of action – being put down/putting oneself down – but the past tense form of one is the same as the present tense form of the other. The confusion is built in and even careful users are likely to have problems with this pair.

To *lay* is to 'put down' and is a transitive verb (i.e. one which is generally followed by an object):

Lay your sleeping head, my love... (first line of poem by W. H. Auden)

To *lie* is to 'be at rest on a horizontal surface' and is an intransitive verb (one which is not followed by a direct object):

He told the dog to lie down at once.

Confusion mostly arises from the fact that the past tense of *lie* is *lay*:

The dog lay down and went to sleep straightaway.

while the past tense of *lay* is *laid*:

They laid the picnic food out on the rug.

The past participle form (i.e. the one used after 'has' or 'had') is *lain* for *lie*:

The farmhouse has lain empty for almost two years now.

and *laid* for *lay*:

The soldiers had laid thousands of mines in the course of the war.

Mistakes like those in the following examples are quite frequent:

The coffin had laid in the chapel overnight... (Independent)

(should be *The coffin had lain...* because after 'has' or 'had' *lie* changes to *lain*.)

Take a rug to lay on and a sheet to shield you from prying eyes. (Sun)

(should be *a rug to lie on* – unless you're a chicken contemplating the production of eggs.)

To *lie* in the sense of 'not tell the truth' takes a different (and regular) past tense/past participle: *He lied in claiming he was elsewhere at the time.*

Embarrassment rating: ●●○○ Although this is a tricky pair to sort out, it can be done with a little care.

How to avoid: Before using *lie* or *lay*, ask yourself which of the two you mean. Then work out whether it refers to an action in the present or past, and follow the *lie-lay-lain* or the *lay-laid* pattern. This is also one of those differences where a sensitive ear to the sound of a sentence can help.

LIBEL *or* SLANDER

These two are often used interchangeably, although there is a difference between them not so much of meaning but of application.

Both nouns and verbs, *libel* and *slander* refer to a 'defamatory accusation' or mean to 'defame'. *Libel* is used about anything written or presented in permanent form, including material on the Internet:

Drudge initially gained his celebrity by libelling me [on a website] on the day I began work in the Clinton White House in August 1997, reporting as fact that I was hiding police records of domestic violence. (Guardian)

Slander tends to be reserved for spoken comments:

Sixteen North Africans... are suing the Spanish prime minister... for slander after he... wrongly claimed they were proof of a dangerous alliance between Saddam Hussein and Osama bin Laden. (Guardian)

Embarrassment rating: ●○○, since the two terms are frequently used for each other. The careful user, though, will want to distinguish between defamatory comments made in print and those which are spoken.

How to avoid: The association between *libel* and anything written is suggested by their shared 'i'. *Slander* is more to do with speech.

LIVID *or* LURID

Both of these similar-sounding adjectives have connections with colour but are most widely used in other contexts. I suspect that their meanings remain a bit hazy, however.

Livid is 'dark', 'leaden':

His cheeks are livid with bruises, although these turn out to be the result, not of the accident, but of dental treatment... (Observer)

but it's most frequently used to mean 'extremely angry' (presumably because of the colour of an angry face). *Lurid* has been used about a range of colour tones, from pale yellow to purple. In another sense it is also a favourite tabloid expression, generally applied now to news stories which have a 'sensational' quality, often but not exclusively sexual:

> *At its peak, tens of thousands would await the latest lurid tales of alien autopsies and flying saucers spying on sleepy market towns.* (Observer)

Embarrassment rating: ●●○ , since the two words don't make much sense if swapped around in some contexts ('I was *lurid* with him'; 'a *livid* story'). However, it would be possible to refer to a stormy sky or someone's complexion as being either *livid* or *lurid*.

How to avoid: When the words are used metaphorically (i.e. *livid* to mean 'angry', *lurid* to mean 'sensational') they need to be kept distinct.

LUXURIANT *or* LUXURIOUS

Both adjectives derive from *luxury* but have distinct meanings which shouldn't be confused.

Luxuriant describes anything which is 'produced in abundant quantities' or is 'lush' – its use is generally restricted to natural growth (hair, foliage, etc.):

> *Seventy-three, but with the luxuriant dark hair of a rather younger man...* (The Times)

Luxurious conveys notions 'of great comfort', expense and (sometimes) flashiness:

> *The house has the self-made man's stamp of being rather too meticulously luxurious to rank as a true grandee's residence.* (The Times)

Embarrassment rating: ●○○ But it would be an error to describe vegetation as *luxurious*.

How to avoid: Roughly speaking, anything which is natural can be characterised as *luxuriant* while items (or surroundings) which are man-made are *luxurious*.

M M M M M

MACHO, MANLY *or* MANNISH

All of these terms relate to masculinity but they apply in quite different contexts.

To take the second word first, *manly* means 'brave', 'fitting for a man'. It isn't used much now, perhaps because it has stiff-upper-lip, Victorian overtones. *Masculine* would be the modern equivalent. *Macho* – from the Spanish word for 'male' – is a rough contemporary version but carries a suggestion of swaggering masculinity which the Victorians would certainly not have approved of:

> *The International Conference was a fairly macho negotiating forum, with a great deal of banging of fists on tables and ripe language...* (Independent)

(*Macho* should be pronounced 'matcho', not 'macko'; the noun is *machismo*.)

Mannish can be applied to women who are considered insufficiently feminine – and for this reason it may sometimes be code for 'gay' or 'lesbian'.

Embarrassment rating: ●●○ Most men would be pleased to be thought of as *manly/macho*, but would not be so chuffed with the description of *mannish*.

How to avoid: *Mannish*, like 'childish' and 'womanish', carries negative overtones.

MAJORITY *or* MOST OF

Both of these very ordinary expressions describe the greater part of something, and there is a tendency to use the first in all circumstances even when the second would be better English.

Majority is a noun meaning 'the greater number':

> *The majority of the people in the poll favoured the death penalty.*

Majority should not be used to mean 'the larger part' of something which cannot be split up into individual elements. When referring to a single unit, *most of* should be used, or another expression such as 'the greater part of':

I was on tenterhooks for the most of the film.

Embarrassment rating: ●◐○ It's quite common to hear references to 'the majority of the film', but this is better avoided.

How to avoid: Only use *majority* when talking numbers or percentages.

MASTERFUL *or* MASTERLY

These two terms deriving from 'master' have an overlap of meaning but can carry different emphases.

The adjective *masterly* means 'highly skilled', 'brilliantly accomplished', and is most often used when a performance of some kind is being praised:

Many will never forget his masterly appearances on TV, smoking the pipe that became his symbol... (The Times)

Masterful is often used to mean the same thing, but it carries overtones of 'bullying', of aggressive assertion, even if this is intended in a complimentary way:

'My camera is often low,' Newton explained, 'because I like the illusion of looking up. I like superwomen, physically strong and masterful.'
(Daily Telegraph)

Sometimes it's not clear whether a writer means *masterful* in this second sense (of 'domineering') or is using it as a synonym for the more complimentary *masterly*, although when applied to performances, films, etc., rather than people, the sense is usually 'highly accomplished':

James Stewart laid his amiable all-American guy persona on the line in Hitchcock's masterful thriller-cum-psychodrama [Vertigo]... (Independent)

Embarrassment rating: ◑○○ These two are often used interchangeably, but there are circumstances in which *masterful* is pejorative and it's as well to be aware of this.

How to avoid: A careful user will tend to apply *masterly* to performances, works, etc. It's worth noting also that some people object to *masterly* as being an inherently sexist term.

MAY *or* MIGHT

There is a growing tendency to use may in all circumstances, even where might would be correct.

May is the present tense form: *We think he may ring.* (But we don't know yet whether he's going to.)

Might is the past tense: *We thought he might ring.* (Either he did ring or he didn't, but the sentence implies that we know one way or the other.)

It would be incorrect to put: *We thought he may ring.* (This doesn't make sense, since the question of whether he rang or not is left hanging in the air, even though the past tense 'thought' indicates that we already know the answer.)

Very generally speaking, *may* should be used when talking about a present or future possibility, and *might* when talking about the past. The following sentence, for example, would read better with *might* since it refers to the past:

*Without the Beatles there may [should be **might**] have been a Bob Dylan, but Brian Wilson would not have written the Beach Boys' Good Vibrations.* (The Times)

However, things are a little more complicated since there are occasions when *might* can be used to refer to future possibilities as in *He might ring*. (This phrasing suggests greater doubt on the user's part than may would do.)

Conversely, *may* followed by 'have' can be used about the past when the speaker or writer is unsure of the situation:

He may have rung; I haven't checked the answerphone.

Might followed by 'have' signifies that something is less likely or no longer possible:

He might have rung if he hadn't been unexpectedly called away.

(In addition, *might have*, used colloquially, can express disappointment or frustration: *He might have rung!*)

Embarrassment rating: ●◑○, since the use of *may* when *might* is required is a very common error. I have a feeling that many people have given up on this one, if they were ever aware of the difference in the first place, and simply grab for *may* whatever the context. All the same, careful users will distinguish between the two.

How to avoid: Quite hard. It takes a bit of thought. As a very rough rule, be wary of using *may* about something that has already occurred.

MEDICAL *or* MEDICINAL

Both of these words are obviously connected to health and sickness but they have slightly different applications.

Medical means 'relating to the practice of medicine' (*medical* student, *medical* insurance) and, as a noun, describes a 'physical examination to check a person's health/fitness':

Beckham, whose lopsidedness emerged during his medical for Real Madrid, is not alone. (Daily Telegraph)

The adjective *medicinal* means 'used in medicine' and so 'helping to cure'. Very often the word has a slightly jokey overtone since it's applied to drinks which are taken for their alcoholic value rather than their supposed 'curative' properties:

> *His father is an alcoholic, addicted to a medicinal concoction of cornflower syrup and turpenhydrate.* (Spectator)

Embarrassment rating: ◑○○ *Medical* tends to be the standard term.
How to avoid: *Medical* treatment is the more general term, covering anything from a visit to the doctor to a session with an osteopath; *medicinal* treatment tends to describe the actual remedies taken for prevention or cure, such as plants or their properties.

MERETRICIOUS *or* MERITORIOUS

These two quite similar sounding words have almost opposite meanings, and the echo of 'merit' in the first word may mislead.

Meretricious has an interesting history since it derives from the Latin word *meretrix* meaning 'prostitute', and indeed its primary sense is 'relating to prostitution'. Never used in this sense now, as far as I can see, it has come to mean 'flashy but without substance':

> *Already this year we have had* Cold Creek Manor, *a meretricious slice of Hollywood slumming from a should-know-better director...* (The Times)

Meritorious means 'worth praising':

> *Being healthy is not meritorious in itself.* (The Times)

Embarrassment rating: ●●◑, in the slightly unlikely event that these two are confused, since a *meretricious* action would be very different from a *meritorious* one.
How to avoid: Meretricious contains almost all of *trick* in its centre and this hints at its meaning, while the beginning of meritorious indicates the sense of this word too.

METAL *or* METTLE

The two are sometimes confused not only because of their identical pronunciation but because ideas of strength and toughness are common to both. Both words/spellings, in fact, have the same origin.

Metal describes 'any of the elementary substances such as gold or iron'. This spelling is sometimes used when *mettle* is meant. The confusion isn't surprising since both words are pronounced the same, and *mettle* carries the metallic-sounding idea of 'hardness', 'spirit'. When people are 'on their mettle' they are put in a situation in which they have to prove themselves:

> *England rugby's men of mettle put on the sort of glistening collective tap dance that takes the breath away.* (Guardian)

Embarrassment rating: ●●◐, since this falls into the category of fairly elementary errors. The mistake, say, of writing about a team's being put on its 'metal' creates an odd image if taken literally.

How to avoid: If associated with verbs such as 'prove', 'show', 'test', the mettle sense/spelling is almost certain to be the correct one.

METER *or* METRE

Both words are to do with measurement, and the slight difference in their endings is a recipe for confusion. In addition, the fact that US usage has only one form for both words (*meter*) makes things more tricky for those Brits who are influenced by American spelling.

A *meter* is a 'measuring instrument': parking *meter*; *thermometer*; *milometer*. A *metre* is the 'basic unit of length in the metric system' (three *metres* in length, a *kilometre* further on). This is the spelling that is also used to describe poetic 'rhythm', the contrasting sounds between long and short or stressed and unstressed syllables in verse.

Embarrassment rating: ●○○ Even careful spellers are likely to be caught out sometimes by this one, and the overall meaning of what you are saying isn't likely to be affected.

How to avoid: A *meter* is a measurer of something. By contrast a *metre* is a unit of distance (note the endings of these words).

MILITATE *or* MITIGATE

These two verbs are often confused because of their similar look and sound but they have nothing in common.

To *militate*, generally followed by 'against', is to 'have weight', to 'operate':
> *The open range of parts he has taken has also militated against the illusion that we, the public, know him.* (The Times)

Mitigate has something of an opposite meaning – it is to 'lighten', to 'make less harsh' (mitigating circumstances in a court of law will reduce the sentence which the defendant would otherwise receive):
> *The best available instrument for mitigating poverty, Wilson decided, was central government.* (Independent on Sunday)

Embarrassment rating: ●●○ These words are slightly outside everyday vocabulary, and anybody using them should be aware of the distinction.

How to avoid: *Militate* is usually followed by 'against' or sometimes 'in favour of', but *mitigate* takes a direct object, as in the example above. You cannot talk about 'mitigating against' something...

MUNDANE or WORLDLY

These two words are an interesting example of the way in which synonyms in English can, on the surface, share the same meaning while possessing different underlying senses.

Both terms mean 'of this world', but *mundane* carries the sense of 'everyday' (to the point of being boring):

Most societies at most times have been happy enough to bind together the idea of prayer with the most mundane, business-like realities of life. (Daily Telegraph)

Worldly is often used as part of compound words ('worldly-wise', 'other-worldly') but it also has a meaning of 'experienced in the ways of the world', 'sophisticated':

Newspaper foreign editors used to know that the person who understood best the heart of an overseas beat was a foreign correspondent's wife; a good one would be worldly in public affairs... (Guardian)

Embarrassment rating: ●●○ Many people would take *worldly* as a compliment but would not like to have their lives described as *mundane*.

How to avoid: *Worldly* should be restricted to individuals or material things ('worldly goods', 'worldly possessions') while *mundane* tends to be used about circumstances, events, etc.

N N N N N

NAKED *or* NUDE

This is quite a difficult distinction – and naturally an interesting one.

Naked is the more versatile word with its senses of 'without assistance' or 'lacking ornament' (*naked* effort, *naked* truth) as well as the basic meanings of 'bare', 'uncovered'. *Naked* is generally a less loaded or emotive word than *nude*, which is probably why it was used in the following story about a child:

> *Police were called to a fashionable art gallery last night when concerns were raised over an exhibition featuring photos of an artist's naked daughter.*
> (Guardian)

Nude has associations with painting, photography and porn, and to that extent it could be equated with being 'intentionally naked' – often for artistic or sexual purposes. Nudism naturally implies a conscious decision to be naked:

> *Japan has a long history of nude public bathing and has only favoured segregated bathing since the end of the Second World War.* (Guardian)

The words aren't quite interchangeable. If you switch round the adjectives in the next example you also alter the balance of the sentence:

> *'I even studied for my own law exams nude to keep the stress down, though unfortunately I wasn't allowed to sit them naked.'* (quoted in The Times)

Embarrassment rating: ●○○ , since there is a degree of embarrassment already built into each word!

How to avoid: Were Adam and Eve *naked* before the Fall, but *nude* after it? More than most differences, this one really is in the eye of the beholder.

NEGLECTFUL, NEGLIGENT *or* NEGLIGIBLE

These words derive from *neglect/negligence* but have moved off in different directions.

Neglectful means 'inattentive', with the implication of failing to care for something or somebody:

His busy life at work made him a rather neglectful father.

Negligent means 'careless', particularly in relation to matters which are your responsibility and for which you may be held accountable. This is a stronger term than neglectful:

I grew up in a world without panic buttons; now an organisation that fails to provide them for its staff is negligent. (Daily Telegraph)

Negligible means 'very slight or unimportant' (and therefore able to be neglected):

Despite all that fuss, the Oscars had a negligible effect on the American box office. (The Times)

Embarrassment rating: ●●○, particularly over the second and third terms. There is a genuine confusion of meaning if, say, an oversight is described as being *negligent* rather than *negligible*, since the implications of the words are almost opposite.

How to avoid: *Neglectful* and *negligent* tend to be used of individuals or groups, while *negligible* applies to events, effects and so on.

NICENESS *or* NICETY

Nice is a very old word with quite a range of meanings. Two of its spinoffs are *niceness* and *nicety*, but in terms of their meaning they are very distant cousins.

Niceness means the 'quality of being nice', 'agreeableness'. There's a blandness to the word or to what it describes, and it's often used with just a touch of criticism:

Being Canadian, the authors have a certain orthodoxy of mind that comes from having lived in a country famed for its niceness. (Daily Telegraph)

Nicety means 'precision' (as when something is judged to a *nicety*) or 'refinement' when it is usually found in the plural form, *niceties*:

[He] concludes that [President] Reagan's crude anti-communism was ultimately much more effective than the diplomatic niceties of more sophisticated politicians. (Daily Telegraph)

Embarrassment rating: ●●○ Swapping the words around in the examples above would produce very different meanings. A person who can display *niceness* in a situation may be totally unaware of the *niceties* of it.

How to avoid: Some manuals on English style suggest avoiding *nice* altogether because it's such a bland all-purpose term, and that might extend to avoiding *niceness* as well. I've always thought that *nice* and *niceness* have had a rather bad press. They remain useful words, carefully used. The same goes for *nicety*. Just remember that this second word has nothing to do with being pleasant...

O O O O O

OBJECTIVE *or* SUBJECTIVE

Both adjectives are to do with point of view. The difference between them is probably plain but for the record...

An *objective* approach is one which is 'unaffected by personal feelings', 'detached':

From an objective angle she could see that the new bypass being built near her house would benefit the whole town.

Subjective means 'personal', 'taking one's feelings into account':

But from a subjective viewpoint she resented the noise and pollution which the nearby road would cause.

Subjective is occasionally used in a critical way, as in 'You're taking a subjective point of view', with the unstated implication that only the speaker is being *objective* and giving an unbiased account.

Embarrassment rating: ●●◐, since the words are opposites.

How to avoid: To be *objective* is to look at matters in an impersonal way (looking at everything, including oneself, from the outside) while to be *subjective* is to regard them from the subject's angle.

OFFICIAL *or* OFFICIOUS

Both of these terms originally derive from the same Latin source but they have very different meanings. The second is sometimes used by mistake for the first, perhaps because people occasionally find that *officials* can also be *officious*.

As an adjective *official* describes a 'person or process that is properly authorised':

the Elysee Palace in Paris, President Jacques Chirac's official residence (Guardian)

The noun *official* is used of someone employed by a government department, as 'senior Pentagon officials'.

The adjective *officious,* by contrast, means 'interfering', with an overtone of fussiness:

'What are you two talking about?' he asked in his usual officious manner.

Embarrassment rating: ●●●, if you describe a person as *officious* when you really mean *official.*

How to avoid: Only use *officious* if you intend to criticise or insult.

ORDINANCE *or* ORDNANCE

The one-letter difference between these two words, and the fact that pronunciation hardly distinguishes between them, can cause problems.

Ordinance – more common in the US than the UK – has the sense of a 'ruling' or 'decree' (especially in a local context):

In the United States of America there are so-called weed ordinances banning lawns over a certain height. (Daily Telegraph)

Ordnance has the general sense of 'military equipment' but is almost always restricted in its application to 'artillery and ammunition':

...the MoD paid out £4.5 million to... tribesmen who claimed to have been maimed or bereaved by live ordnance left over from training exercises in northern Kenya. (Daily Telegraph)

(Ordnance Survey maps are so called because until the end of the 19th century they were commissioned by the Government and produced by its Ordnance Department.)

Embarrassment rating: ●●○ Although *ordnance* grew out of *ordinance,* the two words have moved apart and the mistaken use of one for the other will not convey the writer's meaning.

How to avoid: As indicated above, **ordnance** is probably the more frequent term in the UK – if only because of its everyday appearance on maps of Britain. The connection between an *ordinance* and a ruling might be recalled by the 'i' in the middle of each word.

P P P P P

PEDAL *or* PEDDLE

Identical pronunciation – and perhaps some association between constant movement and door-to-door selling? – cause confusion with these two.

Pedal as a noun describes a 'lever worked by the foot'; as a verb it is to 'operate such a lever':

   I pedalled fast to keep the other bikes in sight.

Pedaller is the associated noun (not very often seen).

   Peddle, a verb, is to 'sell small items'. When applied to any other kind of trade there is the suggestion of sleaziness or illegality: *peddling* lies, *peddling* drugs. Even when it's used in ordinary contexts it tends to disparage what is being 'sold':

   Why don't we stick to the line, peddled by literal-minded idiots, that 'all wine smells of grapes'? (Observer)

(A *pedlar* went from door to door selling goods; the practice may go on but the word has almost disappeared in favour of 'doorstep salesman', etc. The drug pusher or the supplier of doubtful information is a *peddler*.)

Embarrassment rating: ●◐○ Your meaning will almost always be clear even if the wrong spelling is used, except perhaps in a statement like 'I pedalled/peddled my cheap bike' – but the same ambiguity would apply if the words were spoken.

How to avoid: In practice, mistakes are likely to arise over when to use 'pedalled' as opposed to 'peddled', and over the spelling of 'peddler'. Try to remember that *peddle/peddler* always sound pejorative, and rarely if ever apply to the wholesome world of cycling. Otherwise this is one to memorise or, if necessary, to look up before writing down.

PERPETRATE *or* PERPETUATE

These quite similar-sounding words both contain the idea of 'carrying on/out'.

To *perpetrate* is to 'carry out', to 'commit'. The noun that accompanies the verb is often 'crime' or 'outrage' (just as a *perpetrator* is frequently an 'offender', especially in the US where it may be shortened to the slang *perp*). But the context is not always so serious:

> ...*the Academy has honoured some truly unspeakable scenery-chewing performances in the Joan Crawford tradition, mostly perpetrated these days by Mr Geoffrey Rush.* (Spectator)

To *perpetuate* is to 'sustain', to 'make last':

> *She avoids the moral high ground too, and never perpetuates the traditional literary myths of romantic love and happy endings.* (The Times)

Embarrassment rating: ●◐○○ There is a very slight overlap of sense between the two words but a more significant distinction of meaning. To *perpetrate* a mistake is to do it once, to *perpetuate* a mistake is to do it repeatedly.

How to avoid: The link between *perpetuate* and *perpetual* suggests the long-term associations of the first word. Similarly, the connection between *perpetrate* and *perpetrator* helps to clarify the meaning of that verb.

PERQUISITE *or* PREREQUISITE

The similar beginnings and identical endings of these two words may occasionally cause confusion. In addition, both terms describe something which is conditional or dependent.

A *perquisite* is a 'benefit arising from employment'. The word is usually shortened to *perk* – as in 'perks of the job' – and would only be spelled out in full in fairly formal contexts:

> *Among the perquisites of this position are frequent foreign travel and a generous entertainment allowance.*

A *prerequisite* is a 'condition that must be met beforehand':

> ...*cost-effective production and a strong balance sheet are merely the prerequisites for survival.* (The Times)

Embarrassment rating: ●◐○○ There would be a genuine ambiguity of meaning if the 'prerequisites of a job' were confused with the 'perquisites of a job', but, where the second word is not colloquially shortened to *perks*, it tends to be substituted now with a more accessible equivalent like 'benefits'.

How to avoid: A *prerequisite* is a condition, qualification, etc. which is *required*.

PERSON *or* PERSONA

The Latin word for 'person' is *persona* in expressions such as 'persona non grata'. But in English a person and his/her persona are not at all the same thing. What difference is produced by the addition of an 'a' to one of them?

A *person* is just a person, a 'human being' (and the word often carries a slightly dismissive note). But a *persona* (plural personae) is something else – a 'public image', the 'face' assumed when dealing with the outside world' (the term originally comes from the field of psychology but is now widely used in general contexts):

> A former chairman of Granada whose businessman-not-arty-farty-type persona had politicians eating out of his hand, Robinson persuaded Gordon Brown to give money to the arts. (Guardian)

Embarrassment rating: ●○○ In practice, I don't think this confusion is likely to occur but it is useful to be clear about the distinct senses of the two words.

How to avoid: Everybody <u>is</u> a *person*; many people <u>have</u> personas for public consumption. The 'a' in *persona* and public face help to provide a link.

PHENOMENON *or* PHENOMENAL

Both of these words contain a kind of double meaning, and it may not always be clear which is meant.

At its simplest a *phenomenon* is no more than an 'observable event':

> ...bluffing about books is a universal phenomenon. (Observer)

although the word easily shades into its associated sense of 'something extraordinary'. The adjective *phenomenal* is almost always used in this sense and signifies anything 'outstanding':

> Internet bank Egg told a story of two extremes today after a 'phenomenal' year for its UK business was washed away by heavy losses in France. (Guardian)

Although *phenomenal* is often used casually for emphasis, particularly in its adverbial form – as in 'phenomenally boring' – it is preferable, at least in formal usage, to restrict the word to events which are truly 'remarkable'.

Embarrassment rating: ○○○ There's no real embarrassment here and the context will generally make clear which of the two senses of *phenomenon* is intended. And, of course, an occurrence such as a solar eclipse is a *phenomenon* twice over – an observable event but also a remarkable one.

How to avoid: Not applicable.

PITEOUS, PITIABLE, PITIFUL or PATHETIC

Too many closely related words, all connected to the notion of 'pity'. Bear with me, as they say in call centres, while they're sorted out.

The first three adjectives mean 'arousing pity' or 'to be pitied', although with very slight differences in usage. *Piteous* is not applied to individuals as such but to anything that moves us to feel pity:

The searchers heard the piteous sounds of the trapped cat.

Pitiable and *pitiful* can be applied to people and situations. Of the two *pitiful* is perhaps slightly stronger, suggesting someone who arouses pity through some visible means as well as by inner suffering, while *pitiable* is more to do with the latter:

There is moving testimony from the civilian survivors and the equally pitiable aircrew. (The Times)

Both adjectives are also used to indicate mockery (a *pitiful* attempt).

Pathetic has a milder meaning of 'arousing sympathy', but usually carries an overtone, if not of contempt, then of superiority:

Watching a once-admired sports person trying to put a brake on the ravages of time is one of the most pathetic sights imaginable. (Guardian)

The colloquial use of *pathetic* to mean 'useless', or, more casually, as a term passing judgement on an unsatisfactory situation, can sometimes be a source of ambiguity:

There are still oddities like the pathetic minority of women MPs... (The Times)

Here the writer isn't commenting on the quality of women MPs but on the unsatisfactory fact that there are so few of them.

Embarrassment rating: OOO, with the first three since they are pretty well interchangeable, with the qualification that *piteous* tends to be used about sights, situations, etc. rather than directly applying to individuals.

How to avoid: Not much to avoid here although *pathetic* needs to be handled with care, since it can be ambiguous (see above) in a simple phrase like 'a pathetic showing'.

POPULOUS, POPULAR or POPULIST

Three words connected to 'the people' and all deriving from the same source but with distinct meanings.

Populous indicates that an area is 'densely populated' (all cities are *populous* by definition), while *popular* means 'in favour', 'liked by many, or involving many people':

> *Yeltsin was a politician hugely experienced and especially gifted in seeking and, until recently, holding popular support...* (Guardian)

Populist (noun and adjective) generally occurs in a political context and describes 'somebody who aims to appeal to the majority' (by offering to cut taxes, put more police on the streets, etc.):

> *Mr Blunkett, who usually plays the populist to keep control of the centre ground of public opinion, has been the liberal in this instance.* (Guardian)

Embarrassment rating: ●●○ , if the first and second are mixed up, or the second and third. A *populous* place (i.e. a heavily populated one) is not the same as a place which is *popular* (e.g. as a holiday destination) – although, of course, a single spot may be both. Similarly, a *popular* announcement by a politician, if such a thing is possible, would be different from a *populist* one. The first is genuinely welcomed while the second may look like an attempt to curry favour with the public.

How to avoid: Only a place such as a country, state or city can be *populous*, whereas *popular* can apply to people, ideas, musical tastes or decisions. The ending '-ist' often carries a negative taint (as in 'racist', 'sexist'), and *populist* is no exception.

PRECIPITATE *or* PRECIPITOUS

Two similar words, one to do with speed, the other with steepness. Perhaps it is the effect of what would occur to anyone falling over a cliff which produces the quite frequent confusion!

Precipitate, as an adjective, describes an action that is 'rushed', 'headlong':

> *...in the face of this onslaught the British units were in precipitate retreat...* (The Times)

As a verb it means to 'produce abruptly':

> *...the idea that psychological stress can precipitate sudden death...* (The Times)

Precipitous means 'steep':

> *The railway cutting was extremely deep, and unusually precipitous.*

However, *precipitous* is quite frequently used to describe an action which, in strict correctness, should be called *precipitate*:

> *...the precipitous [should be **precipitate**] rush by stores to forsake the high street in return for out-of-town sites...* (The Times)

Embarrassment rating: ●○○ Many people will not detect the mistake and will still get the meaning since the context generally makes it clear. However, there is still some life – and value – in the difference between *precipitate* and *precipitous*, and the distinction is worth preserving.

How to avoid: The sound of each word hints at the meaning: in *precipitate*, the syllables are crowded together, all of them short; in *precipitous*, the word seems to tail away, softly falling out of sight... Failing that, rocks, slopes, and drops are all *precipitous*, and all share a letter 'o'.

PREVARICATE *or* PROCRASTINATE

These verbs sound alike, but I suspect that the two are occasionally confused because doing one of these slightly shifty things sometimes involves doing the other.

To *prevaricate* is to 'avoid giving a straight answer'. Not as outright as lying, it is still evading the truth:

> *When the four-year-old demanded to know why the baby got to sleep with me in my bed, I whimpered and prevaricated...* (Daily Telegraph)

To *procrastinate* is to 'delay', 'put off' (particularly doing something which should be done):

> *[The airline] procrastinated, asked for copies of his tickets, and said it was consulting its office in St Lucia.* (Daily Telegraph)

(The noun forms are *prevarication* and *procrastination*.)

Embarrassment rating: ●◑○ Both terms are critical although, arguably, *prevarication* is worse than *procrastination*. Or should it be the other way round? There's an accusatory ring to both – 'You're prevaricating/ procrastinating!' – and the 'offences' somehow sound the worse for being contained within rather long, Latinate words.

How to avoid: *Prevaricate* contains the idea of *vari*ation or not holding steady and so being evasive; it comes from the Latin verb meaning to 'walk in a crooked or knock-kneed fashion'. As for *procrastinate*, that derives from the Latin word 'cras' meaning 'tomorrow'. As with some other aids to memory, the effort of calling this to mind may be greater than simply remembering the two words.

Q Q Q Q Q

QUASH *or* SQUASH

The second word can almost always be used in place of the first, but the first has a more restricted application.

In a legal context, to *quash* is to 'make invalid' (convictions can be quashed or overturned). It has the more general sense of to 'crush out of existence' but not in a literal sense:

The records were put out in an attempt to quash revived controversy over Mr Bush's Vietnam war-era service in the National Guard. (Daily Telegraph)

Apart from noun senses like 'fruit' and 'ball game', *squash* as a verb has the same meaning of to 'crush flat'. There's a more 'physical' quality to *squash*, which can be used both metaphorically and literally (as here):

Apparently, Wilkinson is cursed with a small entrance to the channel that houses the nerve, squashing it. (Daily Telegraph)

Embarrassment rating: OOO Nil, if one refers to 'squashing a legal conviction'. But high in a reference to 'quashing a nerve'.

How to avoid: Only abstracts – convictions, controversy, etc. – can be *quashed*.

R R R R R

REBOUND *or* REDOUND

These verbs have essentially the same underlying meaning but they are not fully interchangeable.

To *rebound* is to 'spring back'. Even when not used literally, which it generally isn't, the word retains a kind of physical spring:

> *They also had a bitter defeat to rebound from – they played the Soviet team a week before the Olympics in an exhibition and lost 10–3.* (The Times)

To *redound* is also to 'rebound' or 'be reflected back', but this rarer word is found in more dignified contexts. Balls don't *redound*, but words and behaviour do – to your or someone else's advantage, disadvantage, etc:

> *Denis's policy always was to do what redounded to the credit of his wife.* (Daily Telegraph)

Embarrassment rating: ●◐○○ But one shouldn't use *redound* in many contexts. For example, the word would not be correct in the *Times* quotation above.

How to avoid: *Rebound* is usually the safe choice.

RESPECTIVE *or* IRRESPECTIVE

This is not a confusable in the standard sense since problems arise here not so much over the distinction between the two words as over the proper use of *respective* and *respectively*.

Respective means 'with respect to'. *Respective* and its adverbial form *respectively* are generally used when items in two lists are being matched up and indicate that the first item in list a) is paired with the first in list b) and so on:

> *The Specialist, starring Sylvester Stallone and Sharon Stone, as, respectively, an explosives expert and a revenge seeker...* (Guardian)

Respectively has a function here as it makes clear which star takes which role. But the word is often used unnecessarily, as it is here:

...a bemused Inzamam-al-Haq and a clearly irritated Rahul Dravid, the respective captains, were forced to deny that they were playing cricket under orders from their governments. (Daily Telegraph)

(Readers already know this is about India and Pakistan but there's no earlier reference in the sentence to the teams captained by the two cricketers and therefore nothing to connect them to – 'captains' by itself would have done.)

Irrespective means 'without regard to':

Everyone else has to share out anything left over, irrespective of age and closeness to retirement.

Embarrassment rating: ●○○ when *respective(ly)* is used unnecessarily, as in the *Telegraph* excerpt above. Its presence in the sentence is merely irritating, like a piece of grit.

How to avoid: Before using *respective*, ask whether it has any useful job to do in the sentence.

RESTFUL, RESTIVE *or* RESTLESS

All three adjectives derive from rest, and the first and second are sometimes confused even though their meanings are opposed.

Restful means 'soothing', 'tranquil', and is applied, not to people, but to experiences that may have a calming effect, such as listening to a piece of music:

Going on holiday with two young children isn't exactly a restful experience.

Restive describes someone 'twitchy', 'reluctant to be controlled':

The Prime Minister challenged the more restive Tory MPs to accept that Britain had a strategic interest... (Independent)

There is more than a shade of difference between the adjectives *restive* and *restless*. This latter word means simply 'unable to stay still'; unlike *restive* it does not imply that anyone is attempting to exercise control:

These days the black rings [under the eyes] are rarely the effect of all-night partying but more from restless nights with a teething baby. (Guardian)

Embarrassment rating: ●●○ These are very familiar words, even if it's tempting to see *restive* as a synonym for *restful*.

How to avoid: *Restive* and *restless* can only be used of people and animals; *restful* of events and experiences.

S S S S S

SHALL *or* WILL

The difference between these two verb forms is generally sidestepped now, either by shortening both words to *'ll* (I'll, she'll), which buries the difference, or simply by using *will* across the board. But there is a difference...

...which is neatly illustrated by the old story of the two experts on English grammar who drowned. One threw himself into the river intending to commit suicide. To the people standing on the bank, he shouted, 'I will drown and no one shall save me!' The other grammar expert fell in by accident. When he saw that no one was making a move to help him, what he called out was, 'I shall drown and no one will save me!' Yes, I know, this may be a very contrived situation – like a panda walking into a café – but it does hint at the *shall/will* difference.

The distinction between the two is that, when all that is being expressed is simple futurity, *shall* 'should' be used with the first person singular and plural (I/we) and *will* with the second and third persons (you/he/she/they):

I/we shall see you tomorrow.

You/he/she/they will be at the station at 5.30.

The *shall/will* link with particular pronouns is reversed when the sentence contains an element of compulsion or intention or determination: in short, anything that makes it more than a simple statement about the future. In these cases the first person (I/we) takes will while the others are followed by *shall*.

'I will do it, and there's no way you can stop me!'

'You shall go to the ball, Cinderella,' said the fairy godmother.

Embarrassment rating: OOO , for the reasons given above.

How to avoid: In practice these fairly subtle distinctions are no longer observed, although most people would register that, in the 'Cinderella' example above, it is more forceful when the fairy godmother says

'You shall go to the ball...' rather than 'You will go to the ball...'.

SHOO-IN *or* SHOE-IN

There's not much of a trap here perhaps, but there is confusion over which is the correct version of this popular US import.

A *shoo-in* – the term was US slang originally and derives from a rigged horse race – is the 'inevitable winner of a race', a 'sure thing':

> *Thank goodness the laws out there prevent foreigners from standing for President because King Jaw himself, Arnold Schwarzenegger, would be a shoo-in.* (Guardian)

But a different spelling, *shoe-in*, is quite often seen – although, strictly speaking, it is wrong. Interestingly, the mistake, which most likely comes from some association between fitting and shoehorns, may eventually push out the correct version.

> *For all that, the incumbent President is no shoe-in.* (Daily Telegraph)

Embarrassment rating: OOO, since there is apparent disagreement over which is the preferred form of this word.

How to avoid: This is a slightly informal piece of language but increasingly found in written English. The *shoo-in* spelling is still more accurate. Some association between horse races and the 'shooing' sound made to animals indicates the spelling.

SHOULD *or* WOULD

The difference between these two verb forms follows that for 'shall/will' (see earlier entry). It's a minor point of language but quite an interesting one.

Should can be used for the first person singular or plural:

> *I/we should like to thank the speaker.*

while *would* is appropriate for other pronouns:

> *You/he/she/they would have arrived by now but for the snow.*

The tendency is to use would in all cases ('I/we would like to...') and the formulation with should now sounds a little formal though it may be appropriate in some contexts.

Should should, of course, be used when the meaning of 'ought to' is intended:

> *You really should try and see it.*

Embarrassment rating: OOO

How to avoid: *Would* can be used all the time, except where the sense of *ought to* is required.

SIMPLE *or* SIMPLISTIC

A pair of closely related words. There is a temptation to use the second because it 'sounds' better even though the context may not justify it.

Simple has a range of meanings from the positive ('plain', 'unpretentious') to the negative ('gullible', 'silly'). But sometimes *simple* is just too simple to make the right impression, and so we reach for *simplistic*. The two terms are not the same. *Simplistic* means 'naive', 'oversimplified' and is almost always used in a critical sense. A *simple* plan may be a good one precisely because of its simplicity, but a *simplistic* plan can never be good because it fails to take account of the complexities of a situation. Although there's a slightly patronising edge to *simplistic* – since it's applied to other people's ideas and hardly ever to our own – it does carry a meaning which should be kept distinct from the straightforward *simple*:

> *'It's clear from my own work that I believe in a multicultural democracy, but to go from that position to say someone is morally good or bad is either unnecessary or simplistic.'* (quoted in the Guardian)

A lot of people gravitate towards *simplistic* when *simple* would do just as well or even be preferable:

> *And on the most simplistic* [why not **simple**?] *level – the one at which a TV critic necessarily operates – it just didn't compute.* (Observer)

Embarrassment rating: ●○○ People are not likely to pull you up for using *simplistic* – as long as they are not the targets of the word.

How to avoid: If tempted to use *simplistic*, always ask yourself whether it is really justified. It may look good but does it mean anything other than *simple*?

STATIONARY *or* STATIONERY

The endings of these words are pronounced the same, and it is easy to put the wrong one. A classic confusable.

Stationary (adjective only) means 'not moving':

> *The actor then asked the group to move the table with their minds. The table remained stationary, but the actor suggested it was moving.* (Daily Telegraph)

Stationery (noun only) defines the paper, pens, etc. used in a workplace.

Embarrassment rating: ●○○ , because the error may well go unnoticed and the sense will not be affected.

How to avoid: Stationery is what is bought from a stationer's. I suspect that the term has been at least partly replaced by the all-purpose 'office supplies'. So most appearances of this pair of words are likely to be in the *stationary* sense/spelling.

SUGGESTIBLE *or* SUGGESTIVE

Two terms connected to *suggestion* but with widely different uses. Both are slightly pejorative.

Suggestible means 'open to suggestion' and so 'gullible' or 'easily influenced':

> *The hypnotist found some suggestible guests for his next performance.*

Suggestive can mean simply 'evocative' (without defining exactly what is being evoked); often followed by 'of', it can be a feature of more formal/technical writing:

> *In 1859, when the* Origin of Species *had come out, the evidence from fossils was suggestive but very incomplete.*

But *suggestive* generally defines comments which contain a double meaning or have a sexual undertone:

> *The writer was a diffident, ceremonious man unlikely to risk suggestive remarks to his upright publisher.* (Guardian)

Embarrassment rating: ●●○ , since these words convey different notions; and a *suggestive* report could be ambiguous, meaning either *indicative of something*, or just full of innuendo.

How to avoid: *Suggestible* (with the same '-ible' ending as 'gullible') is used of people, often in the context of hypnotism. Applied to remarks and evidence *suggestive* could have a neutral meaning but much more frequently characterises risqué comments.

T T T T T

TEMERITY *or* TIMIDITY

Two nouns which are opposites. It is perhaps the false echo of 'timorous' in *temerity* which sometimes encourages misunderstanding of the first.

Temerity means 'daring', with the suggestion of rashness. It is more usually applied to, say, challenges to authority than cases of physical daring:

The defendant had the temerity to question the sanity of the judge in open court.

Timidity points to an opposite attitude: 'lack of nerve', a shyness that makes its possessor unassertive:

Timidity made him reluctant to speak out even when his own interests were being threatened.

Embarrassment rating: ●●◑, since any confusion gives completely the opposite aspect to whatever is being described.

How to avoid: The meaning of *timidity* is plain enough, but some association between *temerity* and *temper* may help to fix the shared idea of hot-headedness.

THAT *or* WHICH

There's a tendency to assume that these two can be used interchangeably, but this applies only in certain sentence constructions.

That and *which* may be used for each other but only in cases where *which* is not preceded by a comma (i.e. only in defining clauses, not in descriptive ones – see entries for 'which/,which/who/,who' for definition and further discussion). You cannot use *that* in a defining clause. For example, *that* (or *which*) is right in the following sentence:

The city firms that had been invited to tender for the work complained that they had been given too little time.

But it would be wrong if the sentence were rephrased as follows:

*The city firms, that [should be **which**] had been invited to tender for the work, complained that they had been given too little time.*

There are also stylistic reasons for using that simply as a variation on *which*. In the following example, a repetition of *which* within the space of six words is avoided by putting that:

> *...the British and French governments, which own the state railways that in turn own Eurostar...* (The Times)

Embarrassment rating: ●●◐ if *that* is used where it shouldn't be. It may seem pernickety to restrict the use of *that* to defining clauses only... but it's simply correct English!

How to avoid: Since *which* will always be 'right', the play-safe advice would be to stick to that word. That can be used for variation, however. It cannot be preceded by a comma.

TORTUOUS *or* TORTUROUS

Both of these words suggest something unpleasant or worse, and pronunciation sometimes blurs them into one by overlooking the second 'r' in torturous.

Tortuous means 'twisting' or 'highly complicated':

> *We almost got lost on the tortuous mountain path.*

Torturous derives from *torture*, and means 'causing severe physical or mental pain':

> *I spent a torturous hour jammed into the tiny one-man canoe.*

Torturous, in theory a much more literary word, tends to get misused for *tortuous* because of the pain inevitably associated with anything lengthy, complex or laborious.

Embarrassment rating: ●◐○ Both words could be applied to the same thing. Becoming involved in a legal process, for example, might be both a *tortuous* and a *torturous* experience. (In fact an Internet search reveals that the phrase 'tortuous process' has only slightly more hits than 'torturous process', though *tortuous* is undoubtedly what is intended.) However, they have distinct meanings and should not be confused.

How to avoid: The derivation of *torturous* from *torture* is a key to the spelling of this word.

U U U U U

UNDERLIE *or* UNDERLAY

The 'lie/lay' distinction is a recipe for disaster (see relevant entry for an attempt at explanation), and this related pair is no exception.

To *underlie* is to 'lie beneath'. The present participle/adjectival form is *underlying* and the past tense form is *underlay*; the word is normally applied to abstracts such as ideas and principles:

> But September 11 shattered the assumptions that underlay Bill Clinton's world view. (Daily Telegraph)

To *underlay* is to 'lay under' – i.e. to 'place something underneath something else'. The past tense form is *underlaid*. This verb is rarely found, and *underlay* is more often used in its noun sense to describe the 'felt, rubber, etc. placed beneath a carpet'.

Care needs to be taken over the right past tense form of these verbs. 'Underlied' doesn't exist – what the writer of the following meant was probably either *underlined* or some garbled idea of *underlying*:

> For centuries, clergy have from their pulpits been preaching messages that underlied [?should be **underlined**] anti-Semitic sentiment in societies worldwide... (The Times)

Embarrassment rating: ●●○ It's easy to make a mess of this, but the error still stands out even if most readers won't be able to pinpoint exactly what's wrong.

How to avoid: *Underlying* is quite straightforward but the other forms of the word (*underlie/underlay*) are trickier, as are *underlay/underlaid*. Better to avoid this lot altogether unless you're sure of what you are doing.

V V V V V

VALUABLE *or* INVALUABLE

The 'in-' prefix to *invaluable* sometimes causes people to assume it is the negative form of *valuable* (probably by analogy with 'incorrect', 'indecisive', etc.).

The opposite of *valuable* ('having worth') is 'valueless' or 'worthless'. People may occasionally use *invaluable* in this second sense, but its correct meaning is 'not capable of being valued' or 'beyond price' – and therefore very valuable indeed. It tends not to be applied to objects – if the *Mona Lisa* was ever stolen (again) it would be described as priceless, not *invaluable* – and the word is normally coupled with abstract words like 'experience' or 'information':

> He may be 30, but the Welshman's importance to United is still every bit as invaluable as at any time during his wonderful career. (Daily Telegraph)

Embarrassment rating: ●●◐, because to erroneously describe something as *invaluable* when you really mean to say that it is worthless is, in effect, to say the opposite of what you intend.

How to avoid: Remember that 'in-' *in*tensifies *valuable* so that whatever is so described becomes more important than ever.

WWWWW

WHO *or* WHOM

Enter the *who/whom* debate and you enter a little minefield of anxiety, at least for those who are concerned with accuracy. So, when should one use *whom* and – just as important – when should one avoid using it?

Absolutely correct English requires the consistent use of *who* as the subject of a verb, while *whom* is found as the object of a verb or following a preposition:

...it is Gayle King, her best friend, to whom she once gave a million dollars for a Christmas present, who stands in as her sister. (The Times)

(*whom* is the object of 'gave' while *who* is the subject of 'stands')

But it is much more normal to find *who* in speech rather than the technically correct *whom*:

'I'm becoming – definitely have become – as interested in who I work with as what I work on.' (*quoted in the* Independent on Sunday)

Indeed, being 'right' in speech can sound a bit stilted and unnatural:

'Whom are you going to allow to finance it?'

(*quoted in the* Independent on Sunday)

The general use of who, when whom would be grammatically correct, is increasingly common in writing:

When our partners, who [should be ***whom***] *we've sworn never to leave...* (The Times)

...a respected House historian who [should be ***whom***] *Mr Gingrich had summarily dismissed after 12 years' service...* (The Times)

And a large *Guardian* headline (over an article on factory farming) – 'Who's killing who?' – almost certainly opted for the 'wrong' form of the word to avoid the slight fussiness that can sometimes be suggested by whom.

Using *who* when it is the direct object of a verb (as in the last three examples) is more acceptable than using it after a preposition. Here convention definitely favours the switch to *whom*:

...he started with no preconceptions about Mountbatten, about whom he knew little... (The Times)

although it is not hard to find cases that don't follow convention, particularly where the writer is aiming at a conversational tone by putting the preposition after the verb:

...since she minds enough about who you sleep with to want it to be her, exclusively, and for good... (GQ)

If this was the end of the story – with *who* being all right in most circumstances, and *whom* being the preferred form after a preposition such as 'to' or 'about' – then life would be simple. But unfortunately the *who/whom* uncertainty often produces a situation where the attempt to write correct English actually leads to more mistakes. It is quite easy to put *whom* because the construction of the sentence makes it look as though the object form of the word is correct. This tends to occur after verbs like 'think' or 'believe', as in the following examples:

The other's from unmarried friends from way back, whom [should be *who*] *we thought were like us (happily unmarried, but bound by a clutch of deliberate offspring)...* (Independent)

Meanwhile GPs, whom [should be *who*] *the Government assumed were eager to take on hospital work such as small operations, are giving warnings...* (Independent on Sunday)

In each case *whom* is the subject of a verb, and not the object of one, and so *who* should be used:

...unmarried friends... who... were like us... (subject of 'were')
...GPs, who... were eager... (subject of 'were')

The simplest way to establish which form is correct is to recast the subordinate clause as a separate sentence – e.g. 'The Government assumed that they...'. Using 'they' (rather than 'them') indicates that 'who' is right.

The following examples show how it should be done:

Kathy Mitchell... the one who brush salesmen always hope will open the door... (Guardian)

...Czech model Adriana Sklemarikova, who pals said he was set to wed. (Sun)

Embarrassment rating: ●◑○, because the gap between correct usage and what generally happens is wide. But if you put in a piece of formal prose ' This is a person about who...', you are showing either that you don't know the right usage or that you don't care. And there are still people who do know and do care, and they may be the ones reading your words. The reverse error – putting *whom* where *who* is right – is less obvious, but still something to avoid.

How to avoid: Read the advice and guidance given above!

WHO'S *or* WHOSE

Two 'grammar' words, *who's* and *whose*, with identical pronunciation and very similar spelling.

Who's is the contracted form of *who is*. *Whose* is the possessive form of *who*. Although the words sound the same they have completely different functions, neatly illustrated by this line from a play:

"Who's this old relic, whose side is he on?" (quoted in The Times)

The usual mistake is to put the contracted form, *who's*, in the place of the possessive, *whose*, as in these examples:

The Icelandic pop pixie [Bjork], who's [should be **whose**] *new single, Army Of Me, soared into the Top Ten last week...*(Daily Star)

...they too demand to know on who's [should be whose] *side he will be fighting.* (The Times)

Embarrassment rating: ●●● Although this is a mistake we can all make in haste it's still considered by most people to be a major grammatical howler, on a par with confusing *it's* and *its*.

How to avoid: This one is quite hard to forgive as it's so easy to check: just replace *whose* or *who's* by the full-length version, i.e. 'who is'. If this makes sense in the context, then you can use *who's* if you wish. If it doesn't make sense, then the right spelling is *whose*.

Y Y Y Y Y

YIN or YANG

Yin and yang are Chinese terms describing the complementary (but opposed) principles which underlie religion, medicine and so on. The two go together like a horse and carriage – but which is which?

Yang is the 'active male principle', light and warm, while *yin* is the colder and more passive 'feminine principle', each necessary to the other, held in a state of balance and tension, etc. As with various imports from Chinese culture, such as *feng shui*, originally serious ideas have been largely reduced to advertising props or lifestyle adornments for the west:

> How clever of [hotel] owner Anouska Hempel to reflect 'the bi-polarity of the world between yin and yang, black and white, hot and cold...'
> (Daily Telegraph)

Embarrassment rating: ●○○ If you can't sort out your yins from your *yangs*, don't worry – unless you are in seriously New Agey circles. A little face might be saved by ensuring you pronounce *feng shui* correctly (say 'fung shway').

How to avoid: *Yin* contains -i-, as does fem*i*nine: *yang* contains -a-, as does m*a*sculine.

ZZZZZ

ZENITH or NADIR

This is a which-way-round-is-it? difference which, I must confess, is included here partly for the satisfaction of having an entry under 'z'.

The *zenith* is the 'position in the sky directly over the observer's head', and so comes to mean 'high point', 'most flourishing period':

> Evans grew up at the zenith of the Welsh coal industry, when one in four men worked in mining. (Guardian)

The *nadir* is the 'direct opposite of the zenith', and if taken literally would apply to the position under the observer's feet, but it is rarely used in this celestial or astronomical sense and means rather the 'lowest point', the 'worst period':

> The 2002 A-level marking scandal was the nadir, a shambles of control-freakery, pseudo-privatisation and muddle. (The Times)

Embarrassment rating: ●●◑ , since the words convey precisely opposite meanings.

How to avoid: The *zenith* is the high position overhead, the *nadir* is the point under the observer.